Beginning AutoCAD

Beginning AutoCAD

Robert McFarlane MSc, BSc, ARCST, C.Eng, MIMech E, MIEE
Senior Lecturer, Department of Mechanical and Production Engineering, Motherwell College

A member of the Hodder Headline Group
LONDON • SYDNEY • AUCKLAND

To Helen, Linda, Stephen and Sam

First published in Great Britain in 1993 by Edward Arnold
Sixth impression 1997 by Arnold,
a member of the Hodder Headline Group
338 Euston Road, London NW1 3BH

© 1993 Robert McFarlane

All rights reserved. No part of this publication may be reproduced or transmitted in any form or by any means, electronically or mechanically, including photocopying, recording or any information storage or retrieval system, without either prior permission in writing from the publisher or a licence permitting restricted copying. In the United Kingdom such licences are issued by the Copyright Licensing Agency: 90 Tottenham Court Road, London W1P 9HE.

Whilst the advice and information in this book is believed to be true and accurate at the date of going to press, neither the author nor the publisher can accept any legal responsibility for any errors or omissions that may be made.

British Library of Cataloguing in Publication Data
McFarlane, Robert
  Beginning AutoCAD: For Release 12
  I. Title
  005.369

ISBN 0 340 58571 4

Produced by Gray Publishing, Tunbridge Wells
Printed and bound in Great Britain by The Bath Press, Bath

Preface

AutoCAD is the standard draughting package throughout the draughting community. It is very powerful, and allows the user to create drawings after only a few hours of tuition. After the completion of a proper course, most users are proficient in AutoCAD, and with continual practice, will become very competent at producing drawings.

There are many books on the market dealing with AutoCAD. If, like me, you have browsed through some of them, you will have become dismayed at the price and their contents. Most seem to have been written for the experienced user, and very few (if any) for the beginner. My own experience in both education and industry, is that the beginner needs a step-by-step guide on how to use AutoCAD, backed up with exercises which can be attempted after some tuition. Users who are new to AutoCAD are not concerned with 3D, solid modelling, rendering, etc., and worry about a book which only devotes a few chapters to their own needs.

This book has been written for the beginner, but will also provide a good back-up for the more experienced users who have learnt their AutoCAD skills on pre-Release 12 versions. It is aimed primarily at the engineering student, but will also benefit learners in other disciplines.

The book has not been written to cover any specific course, but the contents will meet most of the practical requirements of the City and Guilds 4351 AutoCAD course, as well as the SCOTVEC courses Module 2260120 and HNUnit 2400310. It will also provide excellent material for undergraduates and postgraduates who are following courses which require the use of AutoCAD.

The only requirements for the reader is a blank formatted floppy disk for saving work. I have assumed that the **A** drive will be used, but if your system is set for the **B** drive, then use **B:** where I have used **A:**. Some users may want to save work onto the hard drive, in which case no drive letter need be specified. Users with a directory name should save their work under **\dirname\drgname**.

I have worked through the exercises and tutorials to correct mistakes, but should errors occur, I apologise for them and can assure you that they are completely unintentional.

AutoCAD is fun to use. I have spent many hours using it and am still amazed at what can be achieved. I hope that the reader enjoys working through the book as I certainly enjoyed compiling it. Good luck.

Robert McFarlane
1993

Acknowledgements

I wish to acknowledge the help given to me in the preparation of this book by The Computer Centre in Edinburgh and Millar Currie of Motherwell College.

Contents

Preface v
  Acknowledgments

1. What is AutoCAD? 1
   The main features of AutoCAD
2. CAD system hardware 2
   Input devices   Output devices   Graphics screen   Processing unit
3. Installing AutoCAD 3
   Release 12 requirements
4. About AutoCAD Release 12 4
   Using the book
5. The graphics screen 5
   1. Status line   2. On-screen menu   3. Command prompt line
   4. Drawing area
6. Some AutoCAD terminology 7
7. Dialogue boxes 12
   Scroll bars   Using the dialogue boxes   Editing within dialogue boxes
8. Drawing and erasing 13
   Freehand cursor positioning method   The Erase command
9. Saving, loading drawings and exiting AutoCAD 17
   Saving a drawing   Leaving AutoCAD
   Opening a file (i.e. loading a drawing)
10. Line creation by different methods 20
    Absolute co-ordinate input   Incremental (relative) co-ordinate input
    Incremental (polar) co-ordinate input   Referencing existing entities
    Using AutoCAD's drawing aids   Saving your drawing
    Command entry
11. Circle creation 25
    Centre and radius   Centre and diameter   Two point method
    Three point method   Tangent to two elements and a radius (TTR)
    Saving the drawing
12. User exercise 1 28
13. Object snap (OSNAP) 29
14. Arc creation 32
    Three point method
15. Fillet and chamfer 35
    Fillet   Chamfer
16. Offset, change and LTSCALE 37
    Offset   Change   LTSCALE
17. User exercise 2 39
18. Extend and trim 40
19. Simple text 42
20. Dimensioning 43
    Linear dimensioning   Diameter dimensioning   Radius dimensioning
    Leader dimensioning   Angular dimensioning   The default value
21. Display and view 51
22. Editing: copy, move, rotate, mirror 52
    Copy   Move   Rotate   Mirror   The selection set
23. Grips 62
    Using grips   How grips work
24. Setting the drawing layout 65
    Making a standard sheet

25. Layers — 67
    Linetypes   Layer creation using the on-screen menu and prompt line
    Layer creation using the dialogue box   Saving the standard sheet
    Using layers   Using the standard sheet   Modifying layers
    Changing the prototype drawing name   Layer Locking

26. Adding text — 75
    Text   DTEXT   Text justification   New alignment additions
    Text editing   Modify and entity . . .   DDEDIT

27. Hatching — 82
    The hatch command   Using AutoCAD's existing hatch patterns
    The BHATCH command   Using the dialogue boxes   Exercise

28. The BREAK command — 90

29. Polylines — 92

30. Adding arc segments during PLINE definition — 95

31. PEDIT — 98
    Constant width   Straightening a polyshape
    Fitting a curve to a polyshape   Completion
    Other PEDIT commands

32. User exercise 3 — 103

33. Polygons — 104

34. Control codes for text and dimensions — 106

35. DIMVARS — 108

36. Tolerances and limits — 112
    Lines (a) with dimtp = 0.05 and dimtm = 0.02

37. Arrays — 114
    Rectangular array   Polar array with rotation
    Polar array without rotation

38. User exercise 4 — 118

39. The CHANGE command — 119

40. Text fonts and styles — 121
    Font   Style   Setting styles   Using styles   Using the icon fonts

41. User exercise 5 — 129
    Dimensions and text styles

42. BLOCKS — 131
    Creating a block   Inserting a block   Using erase with a block
    The insert dialogue box   Block exercise   Making the blocks
    Inserting the CAM   MINSERT   *Inserting the followers
    Finishing the drawing

43. WBLOCKS — 139
    Making the WBLOCK   Inserting the WBLOCK

44. Attributes — 142
    Making the attributes   Making the block with the attributes
    The ATTDIA variable   Inserting the attribute block   Attribute example

45. Engineering drawings — 149
    Parts drawings   Assembly drawings   Detail drawings

46. Using the SETUP command — 150
    Large scale drawing   Small scale drawing

47. Point filters — 153

Tutorials 1–44 — 155

1. What is AutoCAD?

AutoCAD is a professional computer-aided draughting (CAD) package which runs on low-cost standard personal computers (PCs). This brings the benefits of a high-performance CAD facility within reach of even the smallest drawing office.

AutoCAD is produced by AutoDESK.

The main features of AutoCAD

1. AutoCAD is a complete, professional CAD system with the power and features of mini- and mainframe systems, costing many times more. It is quick to learn, easy to use and most users can be fully proficient and productive within a couple of months of completing a prescribed training programme.
2. A well-defined menu structure makes the system fast and very efficient to use. Complex command sequencing with user-defined parameters can be activated by a single menu selection, either from the screen or tablet-based menus.
3. Flexibility is the keyword as far as AutoCAD is concerned. The user can define his or her own menus, component and shape libraries, text fonts, line styles, hatch patterns, etc. Command input can be achieved in a number of ways, and in general is very user friendly and forgiving. By utilising the internal AutoLISP package, complex parametric routines can be constructed to eliminate repetitive calculation and draughting.
4. For the 2D draughtsperson, AutoCAD will prove invaluable once the basic concepts have been mastered. Speed of completing an original drawing will be improved, and the editing features are spectacular. Standardisation of dimensions, text, section detail, etc. all provide for a drawing which will impress any client. The fact that very large drawings can be saved on disk for recall, is in itself an amazing feat, and the use of modems means that drawings can be 'transported' quickly and safely to other users wherever they may be.

2. CAD system hardware

In any CAD system, the hardware used can be categorised into four main areas as follows

- the input devices
- the output devices
- the graphics screen
- the processing unit

Input devices

These are generally a *mouse* or a *puck* and are used with the standard computer *keyboard*. These devices are used to input commands and select screen options whilst using AutoCAD.

Output devices

Used to obtain a printed output (*hard copy*) of the drawing They are generally *plotters* although *printers* can be used to obtain a rough output.

Graphics screen

AutoCAD can be *configured* to run with either one of two types of graphic screen arrangement

(a) *dual screen mode*, in which one screen is devoted to text information and one screen is devoted to graphics.
(b) *single screen mode*, in which both graphics and text appear on the one screen, although the user can *flip* between the two types.

The mode used in this book is the *single screen* type.

Processing unit

This is the piece of hardware which does all the hard work in the system. It is within this unit that all the necessary calculations take place, and all the drawings are stored.

This is only a simple introduction to the hardware involved in a CAD system. If further information is required, there is plenty of reference material available for individual reading, although this is beyond the scope of 2D draughting.

3. Installing AutoCAD

The installation of AutoCAD is entirely dependent on company policy, the draughtspeople being 'users only' and will not be involved in any detailed discussions about installation. Individual users should install AutoCAD into its own directory and the installation guide which comes with the package is very comprehensive. Dealers from whom the package has been bought are generally helpful with the installation.

Release 12 requirements

Release 12 requires you to have the following on your PC

- a minimum of 8 Mbytes RAM, although 10 or 11 Mbytes is recommended.
- a hard disk space of 23 Mbytes for the complete Release 12 package (11 Mbytes for the basic level).
- a PC with a 386 processor, although a 486 is strongly recommended.
- a Maths co-processor is *essential*.

4. About AutoCAD Release 12

AutoCAD Release 12 is the latest upgrade to the AutoCAD 'family'. New users will not know of the advancements made in the package, but existing users who are upgrading their skills from earlier versions will immediately become aware of several major changes.

While it is not my intention to list all the changes at this stage, several are worth mentioning

- no Main Menu
- dialogue boxes are used extensively
- ability to external reference WBLOCKS*
- ability to save different dimension variable settings*
- multiple view plotting*
- improved hatching using boundary hatch
- command aliasing*
- layer locking
- plot preview
- additional text alignment facility
- single character text editing
- introduction of grips
- extra editing features when selecting objects.

Most of the above features will be discussed in the book, although several [those marked with an asterisk (*)] are considered slightly more advanced and will not be considered.

Using the book

The book is intended as a self-teaching package for AutoCAD users, and it is important that the reader becomes familiar with the concepts that I have introduced. These are simple, and are

1. User keyboard input and menu selection will be highlighted in bold type, e.g. **@50,200**—keyboard input; **LINE**—menu selection.
2. The AutoCAD prompt will be in typewriter face, e.g. `from point` and `to point`.
3. The symbol **<R>** or **<RETURN>** will be used to signify pressing the return or enter key.
4. The **A:** means that a floppy disk is in drive A.

5. The graphics screen

When AutoCAD is loaded from its directory, the **DRAWING EDITOR** is immediately entered, i.e. the screen on which you will do all your drawings is displayed on the monitor. This screen is divided into four distinct areas (Fig. 5.1) as follows

1. The **STATUS** line.
2. The **ON-SCREEN** menu area.
3. The **COMMAND** prompt area.
4. The **DRAWING** area.

1. Status line

The status line gives the current layer (layer 0) as well as the co-ordinates of the on-screen cursor position relative to the origin. Also appearing on this line is information which relates to the status of functions such as SNAP, ORTHO, etc. There is also a coloured square at the left-hand end of the status line, this indicating the colour of the current layer. The status line is where the pull-down menus are positioned, this giving the status line its other name – the *menu bar*.

2. On-screen menu

The user can select the required AutoCAD command from this area by moving the puck (or mouse) until the command is highlighted in yellow, and then pressing the **PICK** button.

The menu shown in Fig. 5.1 is called the **ROOT MENU** and is always obtained when AutoCAD is first loaded. It can be obtained at any time during a drawing by selecting the word **AutoCAD** from the top of the screen. This word will appear in every menu.

3. Command prompt line

This is where the user communicates with AutoCAD to enter

(a) a command, e.g. LINE, ERASE, ZOOM, etc.
(b) co-ordinate data, e.g. 120,45; @100<45, etc.
(c) other values, e.g. a circle radius of 15.

This line is also used by AutoCAD to communicate with the user, and this could be

(a) a prompt, e.g. enter the circle radius
(b) a message, e.g. entities do not intersect.

If a puck or mouse is being used, the commands selected from the on-screen menus will appear here.

4. Drawing area

The drawing area is the draughtsperson's sheet of paper, and is where the drawing is completed. The origin is at the bottom left-hand corner of the drawing area, and has co-ordinates (0,0).

There is another item on the graphics screen which is worth

mentioning. This is the **UCS ICON** which is displayed at the lower left-hand corner. This icon is an aid to 3D drawing and as such will not be of use in this book. In a later chapter we will discover how to turn this icon off.

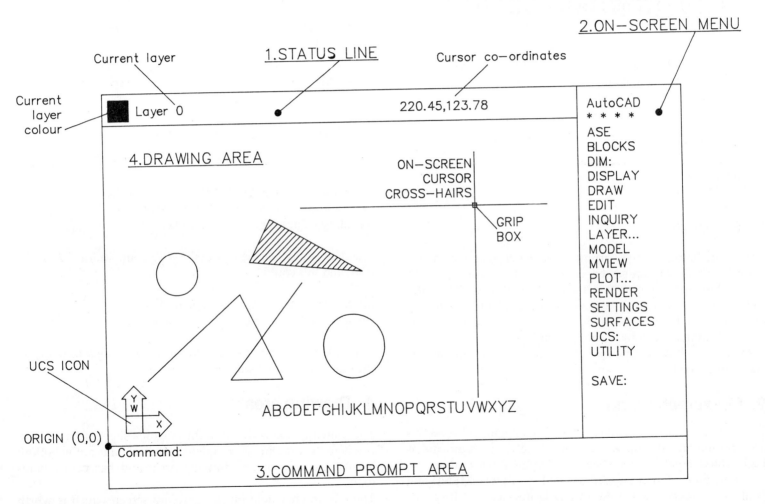

Fig. 5.1. AutoCAD Release 12 drawing screen.

6. Some AutoCAD terminology

AutoCAD has its own terminology, and some of the more common 'buzz' words are listed in this section.

Menu
MENU is a listing of commands. Selecting a menu item may result in (a) another menu appearing on the screen or (b) a command being executed.

Figure 6.1 illustrates how the LINE command is selected from the on-screen menu.

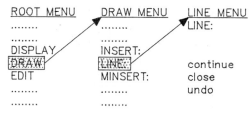

Fig. 6.1.

Key
This is the name for an AutoCAD sub-menu. The DRAW sub-menu is a key, as is the LINE menu.

Command
This is what makes AutoCAD work. A command actually performs an AutoCAD function, e.g. LINE is a command. A command with a colon (:) after it in the menu area is called an *executable command*.

Subcommand
Exists with on-screen menus. These are shown in *lower-case letters* and can only be executed from within a command, e.g. in the diagram above, the word *continue* is a sub-command within the LINE command structure.

Keyboard input
This is when the user types some response from the keyboard. It may be a command (e.g. LINE) or the value of a radius, e.g. 50.

Picking
This is the term for the user to

(a) select an item from a menu
(b) select some line, circle, etc. already drawn on the screen
(c) select a point on the screen.

The puck/mouse is used to 'pick' these items.

Digitise
The phrase 'digitise a point' means 'pick a point on the screen'.

Entity
AutoCAD refers to everything which is drawn on the screen as an entity. Thus lines, circles, arcs, text, blocks, etc. are all entities.

Pointing device
This is a fancy name for the puck/mouse, but it could also refer to a stylus, light pen, etc. The user 'points' the device to

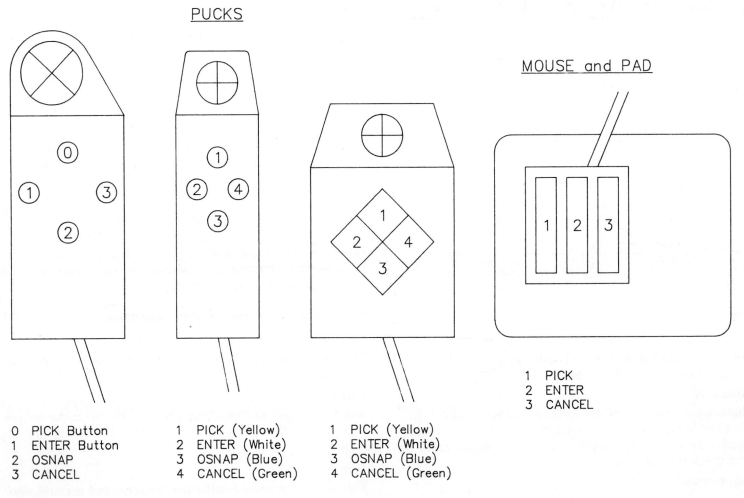

Fig. 6.2. Types of puck and mouse.

an area of the screen and then 'picks' as required. Figure 6.2 (on p. 8) shows three typical pointing devices.

Pull-down menu

These are available for AutoCAD Release 9 onwards and are obtained from the status line or menu bar (see Fig. 6.3). They provide the same information as the on-screen menus but may have additions which are not included in the screen menus. Using the pull-down menus, results in

(a) a command being executed
(b) a following menu appearing
(c) a pop-up menu being obtained with further options for the user.

Figure 6.4 (on p. 10) gives some typical pull-down menus for AutoCAD Release 12, and the diagram below details a typical selection process – often called *cascade menus*.

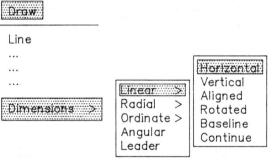

Fig. 6.3. Showing the selection process using the pull-down menus.

Pop-up menu

When certain items are selected from the pull-down or screen menus (those with '...' after the name), a pop-up menu is obtained. By selecting the sequence **Settings, Drawing Aids...,** for instance from the menu bar, the pop-up as shown in Fig. 6.5 (on p. 11) appears.

This type of menu is referred to as a **DIALOGUE BOX,** and the pick arrow is used to activate the required functions.

Icon

This is another type of pop-up menu, specifically used to convey graphical information to the user. The most common icons are used with hatching and text fonts.

Default setting

AutoCAD has certain values (or modes) which are pre-set. For example, the LTSCALE value is preset to 1, while the BLIPS is preset to ON.

These preset values are the default settings, and are shown within angle brackets, e.g. <1> or <ON>. However, the value can be changed by the user if required.

Directory

Areas on the disk where programs and/or files are to be stored are called directories. The AutoCAD program will have its own directory as will other packages which have to be run on the computer, e.g. QUATTRO, LOTUS, etc. Directories can be made with floppy disks, although this is beyond the scope of this book.

Files

With AutoCAD every drawing is called a file, and in computing all files are denoted by a three letter EXTENSION. The drawing files with AutoCAD have the extension **.DWG,** although the user does not require the extension when naming a drawing (sorry file). For instance, DRG1.DWG – computer's name for file and DRG1 – user's name for drawing.

We have now spent enough time talking about AutoCAD without actually drawing. From now on the work will be practically orientated for the reader.

File	Assist	Draw	Construct	Modify	View	Settings	Render	Model	AutoCAD
New...		Line >		Entity...		Drawing Aids...			* * * *
Open...		Arc >				Layer Control...			ASE
Save...		Circle >		Erase >		Object Snap...			BLOCKS
Save As...		Point		Break >					DIM:
Recover...				Extend		Entity Modes...			DISPLAY
		Polyline >		Trim		Point Style...			DRAW
Plot...		Donut							EDIT
		Ellipse >		Align		Dimension Style...			INQUIRY
ASE >		Polygon >		Move		Units Control...			LAYER...
Terminate		Rectangle		Rotate					MODEL
Import/Export >				Rotate 3D		UCS >			MVIEW
Xref >		Insert...		Scale					PLOT...
				Stretch		Selection Settings...			RENDER
Configure...		3D Surfaces >				Grips...			SETTINGS
Compile...				Change >					SURFACES
Utilities...		Hatch...		Explode		Drawing Limits			UCS:
Applications...		Text >							UTILITY
		Dimensions >		PolyEdit					
About AutoCAD...									SAVE:
Exit AutoCAD				Edit Dims >					

NOTES:
1. Selecting items with ... may mean a wait the first time they are picked. This is because they must be 'initialised' by AutoCAD.
2. Items marked with a > mean that there is a following menu.
3. Items with ... mean that a pop-up menu will result.
4. Items which are in 'light text' mean that they are not available.
5. Items with nothing attached are directly executable.

The PICK ARROW used for selection.

Command:

Fig. 6.4. AutoCAD Release 12 pull-down menus, with File, Draw, Modify and Settings in full.

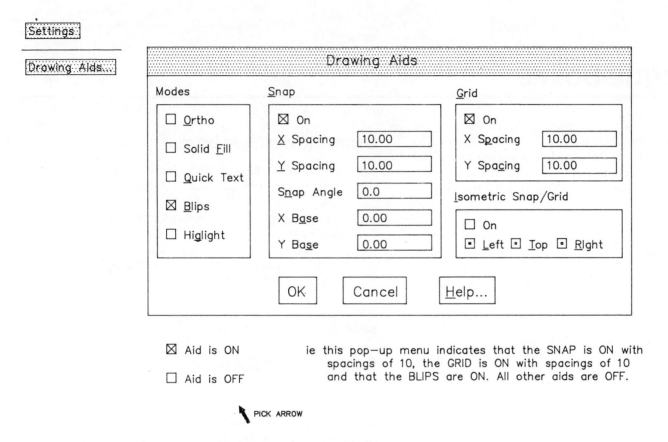

Fig. 6.5. Selection using the pop-up menu.

7. Dialogue boxes

Many AutoCAD commands result in a dialogue box appearing on the screen. While these dialogue boxes are used for different purposes, the general layout and usage is the same for each. Most dialogue boxes are divided into two distinct sections

Directories
AutoCAD directories and sub-directories.
Drives A, B, C.

Files
Selection of items contained in directories and drives, e.g. drawings, text files, etc.

Scroll bars

Dialogue boxes contain a scroll bar for moving through a list of items for selection. The up and down arrows are used to scroll on one item at a time, while the slide box is used to display items 'further up/down' the list (see Fig. 7.1).

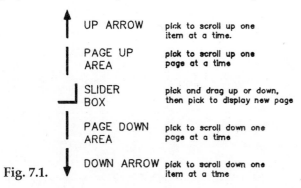

Fig. 7.1.

Using the dialogue boxes

All dialogue boxes have a 'pick-arrow' which the user positions over the item to be selected, and then

1. Pick the item (or 'click' on it) with the pick button on the pointing device.
2. The selected item should turn blue.
3. (a) Pick on it again (called 'double clicking').
   or (b) press <RETURN>.

When dialogue boxes are used in the book, I will discuss in detail the selection methods.

Editing within dialogue boxes

AutoCAD allows text within a dialogue box to be edited. The pick arrow is used to position the cursor (a vertical line |) inside the text to be edited, and 'clicked' into position. Text can then be edited as follows

display	*response*	*result*	
ME|T	enter E	MEE|T|	cursor position
TE|EN	backspace	T|EN	
Auto|CAD	<	Aut|oCAD	
Auto|CAD	>	AutoC|AD	
Auto|CAD	delete	Aut |CAD	

8. Drawing and erasing

As stated in the previous chapter, AutoCAD refers to all lines, circles, text, etc. as *entities*. The simplest entity to draw is a line, and all lines require a start point (*from point*) and an end point (*to point*).

There are a number of different ways of defining these start and end points

- by freehand cursor positioning
- by **absolute** co-ordinate input
- by incremental (**relative**) co-ordinate input
- by incremental **polar** co-ordinate input
- by referencing existing entities
- by utilising drawing aids such as GRID, SNAP and ORTHO.

Freehand cursor positioning method

Let us assume that you have loaded AutoCAD and entered the Drawing Editor. We are now going to draw some lines and circles on the screen, so select from the on-screen menu

> DRAW
> LINE

Now observe the command prompt. AutoCAD is asking for the start point of the line, i.e. the *from point*. Position the cross-hairs of the on-screen cursor as required and press the **PICK** button on the puck/mouse.

Observe the command prompt line again. AutoCAD is now asking for the end point of the line, i.e. the *to point*. Position the cursor at a different point on the screen and press the **PICK** button. This is your first line drawn with AutoCAD.

The command line is again asking for an end point; it has assumed that you will be continuing to draw a line from the end point of the first line drawn. Continue to draw a series of interconnected lines by 'picking' new end points on the screen. Note the *rubberband* effect as the lines are '*drawn out*'. This effect is obtained with all entities drawn on the screen, and with the edit commands. When you have drawn enough lines, press the **ENTER** button on the puck/mouse, or enter <RETURN> from the keyboard. Try and draw some extra lines of your own.

Now select from the screen menu

> DRAW
> CIRCLE
> CEN,RAD

Try and draw a few circles, remembering that a circle needs a centre point (CEN) and a radius (RAD). Figure 8.1(a) gives a typical screen plot of lines and circles drawn using this method of freehand positioning.

The Erase command

Before moving on to the next option of line creation, we will investigate how to delete some (or all) entities from a drawing. This is achieved by using the **ERASE** command.

Erasing single entities

Select from the screen menu

**EDIT
ERASE**

AutoCAD prompts by asking you to *select objects*, i.e. the entities you wish to erase from the drawing. This is achieved by selecting the desired lines and/or circles individually, by positioning the small box attached to the cross-hairs of the cursor on top of the entity to be erased and pressing the **pick** button. The selected entity will change appearance. Repeat this selection process for every entity to be erased, and then press the **ENTER** button on the puck, or the **<RETURN>** key on the keyboard. The entities selected should have disappeared. Figure 8.1(b) demonstrates this method of erasing.

Now draw some other lines and circles on the screen.

Erasing with window/crossing

Selecting single entities for erasing is satisfactory if there are only a few to be removed. When a large number of entities require removal, the single entity selection method can be very tedious, and AutoCAD overcomes this by enabling the user to position a *'window'* over an area of the screen. This erases several entities at the one 'pick'.

To demonstrate the window effect, select **ERASE** from the screen menu and then enter **w<R>** at the prompt line. AutoCAD now asks you to pick *two diagonally opposite corners* of a rectangle. Respond by picking as required, referring to Fig. 8.1(c). All entities that are *completely enclosed* within this defined rectangle will be highlighted, and erased when the **<RETURN>** button is pressed on the keyboard or puck.

Now draw some more lines and circles, then select **ERASE** and enter **c<R>** at the prompt line. Position a window as before and then press **<RETURN>**. Note the entities that have been erased. Figures 8.1(c) and (d) show the difference between the window and crossing selection, this being that window – entities completely enclosed in window are erased and crossing – entities which are enclosed and which cross the window are erased.

Before leaving this chapter, I would like to discuss the ERASE command in depth as some important points can be made which affect other commands. The complete ERASE command is

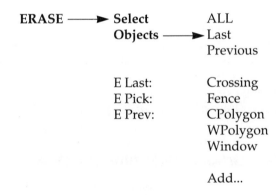

1. **E Last** will erase the last entity drawn, and does not require the **<RETURN>** button to be pressed.
2. **E Pick** allows the user to select single entities for erasing, and does not require **<RETURN>**.
3. Crossing and window are selected with

**ERASE
Select objects
crossing/window**

14 *Beginning AutoCAD*

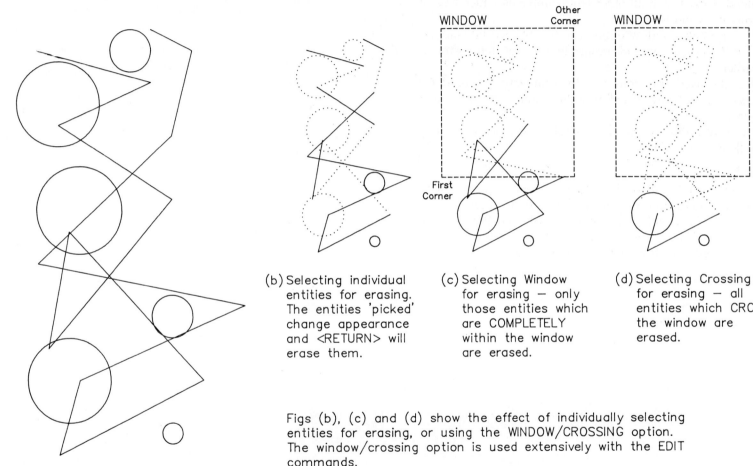

(a) Using the puck/mouse to draw lines and circles.

(b) Selecting individual entities for erasing. The entities 'picked' change appearance and <RETURN> will erase them.

(c) Selecting Window for erasing — only those entities which are COMPLETELY within the window are erased.

(d) Selecting Crossing for erasing — all entities which CROSS the window are erased.

Figs (b), (c) and (d) show the effect of individually selecting entities for erasing, or using the WINDOW/CROSSING option. The window/crossing option is used extensively with the EDIT commands.

Fig. 8.1. Drawing and erasing entities.

4. The **Select objects** option shown with the ERASE command is used with all other edit commands which have a crossing/window option.
5. The crossing/window option can be obtained by entering **C** or **W** at the command prompt line, as was demonstrated earlier.
6. It is the user's preference as to what option is used for selecting the window, i.e. from the menu, or from the keyboard.
7. The **Select objects** has other useful editing facilities which will be discussed later.

Note

It would be advisable for the reader to spend some time with the ERASE menu and become familiar with its usage. Do this by drawing lines and circles on the screen and then use the different ERASE options available, observing the effect of each. This will greatly assist you in future work.

9. Saving, loading drawings and exiting AutoCAD

It is essential that the user knows how to save drawings to disk and how to recall drawings which have been previously saved. Without this ability it is not possible to use AutoCAD properly. It may not be possible to complete a drawing at the 'one sitting' and the drawing must therefore to stored on disk for future recall.

Make sure you are in AutoCAD and have some lines and circles drawn on the screen. This will be our 'completed drawing' which is to be saved to disk, so ensure you have a formatted floppy in the A drive.

Saving a drawing

Select from the menu bar

> **File**
> **Save As...**

A pop-up dialogue box will appear similar to that shown in Fig. 9.1. This dialogue box is used extensively when drawings are to be saved and loaded from disk.

1. Check the *Pattern name* box. Drawings are stored with the file extension **.dwg**, and this is what we want to appear here. If *.dwg does not appear in the pattern name box, position the arrow at the right hand end of any text and press the pick button. Now use the 'backspace' key to delete the text, and then enter *.dwg <R>. This will then set the dialogue box for drawing files.

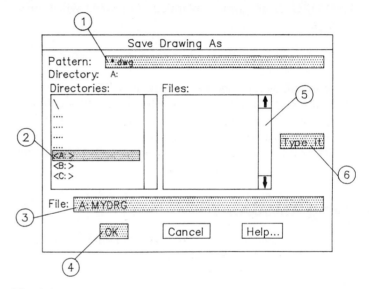

Fig. 9.1.

2. Position the pick arrow over the **A:** in the *Directories* column. The A: should be highlighted in blue, and when it is, press the **<RETURN>** key. This will list all the drawing files which are on floppy disk in the A drive. The list will appear in alphabetical order in the Files column. At present you should not have any file names in this column, as you have not yet saved any drawings. Also note that **A:** appears in the second row.

3. Now position the pick arrow in the File name box and

Saving, loading drawings and exiting AutoCAD **17**

press the pick button. A vertical line will appear, indicating that this row is now active. Enter the name of the drawing, e.g. **A:MYDRG**. The A: is not really needed, as we have specified that the A drive is to be used (step 2), but it will not do any harm to enter it.
4. Pick the OK box, and the drawing should be saved as **A:MYDRG**. If all goes as planned, AutoCAD will return the message

```
Current drawing name set to A:MYDRG
```

and you will be returned to the drawing editor.
5. There are two arrows in the directories and files column, which are used to 'scroll' up or down if the number of files exceeds what can be shown in the box.
6. The **Type it** box allows the user to enter the drawing name to be saved at the command prompt line.

Leaving AutoCAD

There are two ways with which to end a drawing session and leave AutoCAD, either by selecting **Exit AutoCAD** from the File menu or by entering QUIT at the command prompt line.

Select **File** from the menu bar, then **Exit AutoCAD**. You should be returned to the directory from which AutoCAD was loaded.

Opening a file (i.e. loading a drawing)

Reload AutoCAD, and when the drawing editor appears, select from the menu bar

        File
        Open...

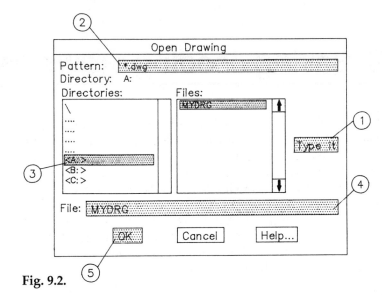

Fig. 9.2.

The **Open** drawing dialogue box will appear, similar to that shown in Fig. 9.2.

1. A drawing can be loaded by picking the **Type it** box, and entering the drawing name at the command prompt line, e.g. **A:MYDRG**. Leave this option for the present. You can try it yourself later.
2. Check that *.dwg appears in the *Pattern* box. If it does not, use the method described in the save section to enter it.
3. Pick **A:** from the *Directories* column and press **<RETURN>**. This will then list all drawings on the floppy in drive A.
4. Position the pick arrow over the drawing to be loaded, and it will be highlighted in blue. When it is, press the **pick** button. You should only have **MYDRG** listed.
5. The drawing name selected will appear in the *File name* box.

18 *Beginning AutoCAD*

6. If this is the correct drawing, pick the *OK* box and the drawing will then be loaded into the drawing editor for you to work on.

The procedures described for saving and loading drawings may seem laborious to the user, but they become second nature after a short time. The dialogue boxes have many advantages over earlier releases, especially in allowing the user to 'see' all drawing files in a directory, or contained on a floppy.

❏ **Summary**

Saving
1. Select File then Save As... from menu bar.
2. Ensure *.dwg name is in Pattern box.
3. Pick A: from directories list.
4. Enter drawing name at File box.
5. Pick OK box.

Loading
1. Select File then Open... from menu bar.
2. Check *.dwg is in Pattern box.
3. Pick A: from directories list.
4. Pick drawing name from Files list.
5. Ensure correct drawing name is in File name box.
6. Pick OK box.

Leaving AutoCAD
1. Select File then Exit AutoCAD from menu bar. Always save before you exit.
2. When the Exit AutoCAD option is selected, a dialogue box similar to that shown below may appear. This occurs if you leave a drawing which has had some changes made to it. AutoCAD will warn you that these changes have not been saved, and you can

(a) select the Discard Changes box and quit AutoCAD
(b) select the Save Changes, in which case you will be asked for a drawing file name.

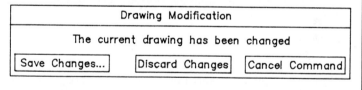

10. Line creation by different methods

The lines created in Chapter 6 were drawn at random with no attempt being made to draw to a specific length. To draw lines accurately, we utilise co-ordinate input for the start and end points of the line. Co-ordinate input can have different forms, and each will be discussed in turn.

Load AutoCAD if you have left it, or make sure that you have a blank screen–erase any entities from it. Now refer to Fig. 10.1, and we will draw the five 50 unit squares shown.

Absolute co-ordinate input

This means that all co-ordinates are taken from the origin at the bottom left-hand corner of the drawing area. The origin has co-ordinates of (0,0) and the normal X–Y axis system is used. Select from the screen menu

>   DRAW
>   LINE

AutoCAD prompts for a start point and an end point for each line to be drawn. In response to each prompt, enter the following, pressing <RETURN> after each entry

```
From point  50,50       the start point
to point    100,50
to point    100,100
to point    50,100
to point    50,50       to complete the square
to point    RETURN      to end the sequence.
```

Incremental (relative) co-ordinate input

This takes co-ordinates from the *last point* entered on the screen, and uses the @ symbol to obtain this. Repeat the LINE command by either (a) selecting **LINE** from the menu, (b) pressing the **ENTER** button on the puck/keyboard or (c) entering the word **LINE <R>** from the keyboard.

In response to the `from point` and `to point` prompts, enter the following

```
From point  150,50      the start point
to point    @50,0
to point    @0,50
to point    @-50,0
to point    @0,-50      to complete the square
to point    RETURN      to end the sequence.
```

Incremental (polar) co-ordinate input

Co-ordinates are again relative to *last point* entered, but uses angular input, so repeat the **LINE** command, then

```
From point  175,150     the start point
to point    @50<45
to point    @50<135
to point    @50<225
to point    @50<-45     to complete the square
to point    RETURN      to end the sequence.
```

Beginning AutoCAD

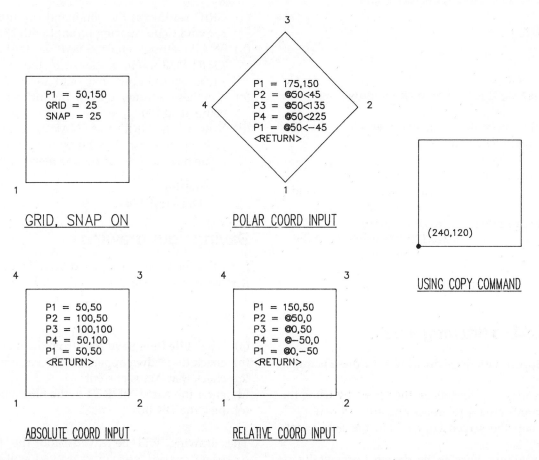

Fig. 10.1. Line creation by different methods: (a) absolute co-ordinate entry, (b) relative co-ordinate entry, (c) polar co-ordinate entry, (d) grid and snap and (e) using the copy command.

Referencing existing entities

When any shape has been drawn it can be exactly copied to any other point on the screen. This is achieved by using the **COPY** command, so select from the screen menu

>   **AutoCAD**
>   **EDIT**
>   **COPY**
>   (a) **enter w <R>** or
>   (b) **pick Select Objects then pick window.**

In response to the prompts, completely window the *first square* drawn and press **RETURN.**

>   AutoCAD prompts: Base point
>   enter: **50,50**   (the lower left-hand corner of square).
>   AutoCAD prompts: Second point
>   enter :   **240,120** (co-ordinates of the newpoint).

The square should be copied to the new position.

Using AutoCAD's drawing aids

AutoCAD is equipped with three drawing aids, these being

- GRID – puts a series of grid dots on the screen by using the F7 key. These points are for reference and are 'not real'.
- SNAP – will snap the screen cursor onto the grid points (F9).
- ORTHO – only allows lines to be drawn horizontally or vertically with the F8 key.

The F7, F8 and F9 refer to the **FUNCTION** keys which **TOGGLE** the aid 'on' and 'off'. Press F7 a few times and a grid will appear. If F8 and/or F9 is pressed, the word ORTHO/SNAP will appear in the STATUS line.

(a) GRID setting: at the command prompt, enter **GRID** and respond to the spacing prompt with **25<RETURN>**.
(b) SNAP setting: enter **SNAP** at the prompt line, then **25<RETURN>** in response to the spacing prompt. The cursor should now 'snap onto' the grid points.
(c) Use these settings to draw the fifth square, the start point being at **50,150**.
(d) Now set the GRID and SNAP back to the original setting of 10 in each case. Try this by using the Drawing Aids dialogue box, i.e. select from the menu bar

>   **Settings**
>   **Drawing Aids...**

Saving your drawing

Now that you have completed your first AutoCAD drawing, it must be saved on disk, as it will be used for future work. The save sequence was covered in the last section, but we will review it here, so

(a) select **File** then **Save As...** from the menu bar
(b) check that ***.dwg** appears in the Pattern box
(c) check that **A:** is current
(d) enter the name **A:DRG1** in the file name box
(e) pick the **OK** box.

The drawing will be saved, and the message `Current drawing name set to A:DRG1` will appear at the command prompt line.

❏ *Summary*

1. Co-ordinate input can be *absolute, relative* or *polar*
2. ABSOLUTE is from the origin – the point (0,0). Positive directions are UP and to the RIGHT, negative directions are DOWN and to the LEFT.
3. RELATIVE refers co-ordinates to the *last point* entered, and uses the @ symbol to achieve this. The entry format is **@30,40**. The 30 is the horizontal distance and the 40 is the vertical distance from the last point entered.
4. POLAR also refers co-ordinates to the *last point* entered. The @ symbol is used, the format being **@50<34**. The 50 is the length of the line being drawn, and 34 is the angle of the line relative to the datum (i.e. the 3 o'clock position). Note that there is *no comma* with this format and an angle of −45° is the same as an angle of +315°.
5. It is possible to use all three input methods concurrently, so try the following sequence

```
LINE from point   100,100      the start point
to point          200,200      ABSOLUTE entry
to point          @-100,0      RELATIVE entry
to point          @100<-45     POLAR entry
to point          RETURN.
```

Note the effect, and then ERASE the three lines.

6. Certain FUNCTION keys are used for drawing aids. These are

    F1 – toggles between the text and graphics screen.
    F6 – co-ordinates
    F7 – grid
    F8 – ortho
    F9 – snap.

Notes

1. The drawing aids can be activated by either (a) using the dialogue box and entering the required values or (b) entering the word and value at the prompt line.

    The user should make up their own mind on how to set these, but my preference is to use the prompt line, e.g. entering SNAP then 5.
2. When a command has been completed, and you want to use it again immediately, it is not necessary to select the command from the menu. Selecting the item from menu is not wrong, but by pressing the **<RETURN>** button on the puck or keyboard, you can re-enter the last command, i.e. *pressing the **<RETURN>** button (puck or keyboard) will restore the last command.*
3. Using the @ key *on its own* will snap the cursor to the last point referenced.

Command entry

Several AutoCAD commands have already been used, e.g. LINE, ERASE, etc. and all commands can be 'activated' by different methods

1. By typing the required command at the prompt line. This needs the user to know all the commands by name.
2. By using the **INS** key and the four cursor control key to move up and down the menu. This is very slow and is only for users who have no puck/mouse.
3. From the on-screen menu by 'picking' the required item.

4. From the menu bar.
5. By using a calibrated tablet.

I will mainly use option (3), i.e. commands will be selected from the on-screen menus, although options (1) and (4) will also be used. The tablet menu will *not* be used.

Activity

Believe it or not, you are now in the position to try some drawings for yourself. These are Tutorials 1 and 2 which only require the LINE and CIRCLE commands. Make sure that your screen is clear and proceed with the drawings noting

- *Tutorial 1:* the shapes have to be to your own sizes, and the drawing aids GRID and SNAP should be ON. When complete, use the **Save As...** option with the file name **A:TUT1**.
- *Tutorial 2:* this requires the user to draw three different shapes on the one drawing. Absolute, relative and polar co-ordinate entry will be required, but the only command is LINE. Save as... **A:TUT2**.

11. Circle creation

AutoCAD offers five different methods of drawing circles. These are

- the centre and radius method
- the centre and diameter method
- two diametrically opposite points on a diameter
- any three points on the circle circumference
- specifying two tangent points and a radius.

Referring to Fig. 11.1, we will draw circles with each method. If you are still in AutoCAD with the drawing of the five squares, then continue as below. If not, then use the **Open...** option with the file name **A:DRG1** to load the drawing.

Centre and radius

Select from the screen menu

DRAW
CIRCLE
CEN,RAD

AutoCAD prompts	Centre of circle
enter	**75,75<R>**
AutoCAD prompts	Radius
enter	**20<R>**

Centre and diameter

Select from the screen menu

DRAW
CIRCLE
CEN,DIA

AutoCAD prompts	Centre of circle
enter	**175,75<R>**
AutoCAD prompts	Diameter
enter	**20<R>**

Two point method

This method requires two points at opposite ends of the circle diameter, so select

DRAW
CIRCLE
2 POINT

AutoCAD prompts	First point on diameter
enter	**55,175<R>**
AutoCAD prompts	Second point on diameter
enter	**95,175<R>.**

Three point method

Select from the menu

    DRAW
    CIRCLE
    3 POINT

AutoCAD prompts for you to define three points on the circle circumference. Respond to each prompt by **picking** points at random as shown by d1, d2 and d3 in Fig. 11.1.

Tangent to two elements and a radius (TTR)

Select from the menu

    DRAW
    CIRCLE
    TTR

AutoCAD prompts	`Enter Tangent spec`
respond	**by picking line A**.
AutoCAD prompts	`Enter second Tangent spec`
respond	**by picking line B.**
AutoCAD prompts	`Radius <?>`
enter	**15<R>**

Note that the circle drawn does not touch the two lines A and B. AutoCAD 'assumes' that the lines are continuous, and draws the circle accordingly.

    Now repeat the TTR method, picking lines C and D in reply to the prompts. The radius is to be 25.

Saving the drawing

Save the drawing at this stage, using the **Save As...** option, but keep the same name, i.e. **A:DRG1**. Now **Exit AutoCAD** or proceed to the activities below.

❏ *Summary*

1. Circles can be drawn in different ways, the most common being the CEN,RAD method.
2. The TTR method can be used with any two entities, i.e.

    (a)   two lines,
    (b)   two circles,
    (c)   a line and a circle or,
    (d)   a line and an arc, etc.

3. The centre point can be obtained (a) by entering co-ordinate data from the keyboard, (b) by picking a point on the screen or (c) by using the OSNAP command (described later) and referencing entities already drawn on the screen.
4. The radius can also be obtained by the methods listed above.

Activity

Attempt Tutorial 3, which consists of lines and circles. It can be drawn using the commands already used, i.e. LINE, CIRCLE and ERASE. Save the drawing as **A:TUT3**.

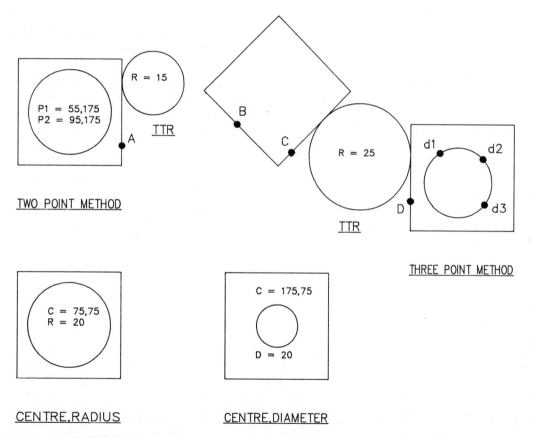

Fig. 11.1. Circle creation using different methods: (a) centre, radius, (b) centre, diameter, (c) two points on diameter, (d) three points on circumference, (e) tangent, tangent, radius (TTR).

Circle creation 27

12. User exercise 1

Load AutoCAD and then

1. Select **File, New...** from menu bar.
2. Enter **A:WORKDRG** in New Drawing Name box.
3. Pick the **OK** box.

This means that we will begin a new drawing with the name stated.

WARNING: Do not alter the ACAD prototype drawing name.

Draw full size the shape shown using the given sizes. *Do not* attempt to add dimensions. The start point at the bottom left-hand corner has co-ordinates (50,50). Use (a) relative co-ordinate entry to draw the outer profile and (b) absolute co-ordinate input (i.e. from the origin) to obtain the circle centres.

When the drawing is complete use the **Save As...** option to save the drawing for future work. The name entered at the start, i.e. **WORKDRG** should be in the File name box, and you should only have to pick the OK box to save the drawing. Alternatively, you could use the **Save** option which will save the drawing without the dialogue box. I prefer to use the **Save As...** option, as it gives me a bit of control over the drawing names.

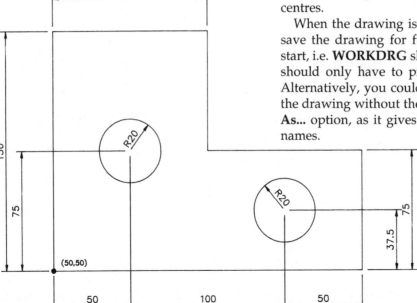

Fig.12.1.

13. Object snap (OSNAP)

There are a number of OSNAP qualifiers used in AutoCAD, and they allow the user to reference points on existing entities, e.g. lines, circle, arcs, etc. This greatly facilitates the creation of new entities. With OSNAP we can tell AutoCAD that we want to draw a line from the end of an existing line, to the midpoint of another line, or that we want to draw a circle whose centre point is at the intersection of two lines already drawn.

The OSNAP menu can be activated in several ways

1. By selecting **** from the screen menu.
2. By selecting **Assist** then **Object Snap** from the menu bar.
3. By pressing the **OSNAP (BLUE) button** on the puck, if it is available.

My preference is to select OSNAP from the screen menu, i.e. '****'. The OSNAP options available are

CENtre	NEArest
ENDpoint	NODe
INsert	PERpendicular
INTersection	QUAdrant
MIDpoint	TANgent.

We will illustrate the use of OSNAP by using the drawing with the circles and squares, so **Open...** with the file name **A:DRG1**.

Before proceeding with the exercise, a general point of interest about OSNAP. With OSNAP the user picks entities using an *Aperture box*, and the size of the box can be set by the user. If the box size is too large, then it is possible that more than one entity will be selected when picking. To ensure that this does not happen, we will set the size of the box to three units, with the following sequence

AutoCAD
SETTINGS
Apertur:
3

Now refer to Fig. 13.1, and delete the two circles *not inside squares*.

Select from the screen menu

DRAW
LINE
****
ENDpoint.

AutoCAD prompts   `from ENDpoint of what line`
respond   **by picking line d1 at the right-hand end.**
Respond to the `To prompts` with the following sequence

****
MIDpoint
pick line d2

Object snap (OSNAP)   29

```
****
PERpend
pick line d3
****
CENtre
pick circle d4
****
QUAdrant
pick circle d5
****
TANgent
pick circle d6
****
QUAdrant
pick circle d7.
```

Now repeat the '****' commands and try to finish the rest of the lines as shown in Fig. 13.1. The OSNAP commands and the lines to pick are all stated in the drawing.

When complete, save the drawing as **A:DRG1**.

Notes

1. The user should by now be reasonably proficient at selecting items from the menu and using the puck/mouse to draw. When entities are drawn, you will have noticed that small 'crosses' are added at the end points of lines, arcs, etc. These are called *blips* and new users to AutoCAD can become confused with them. They are *not entities* and therefore cannot be erased, but can be cleared from the screen by a simple sequence: (a) by selecting **View** the **Redraw** from the menu bar and (b) by entering **REDRAW<R>** at the command prompt line. Later on we will find out how these blips can be 'turned off'.

2. A point worth mentioning at this stage of the learning process, is the use of the **CONTROL C** keys. If you are ever 'in trouble' when drawing, e.g. cannot get out of a command sequence or a menu selection, then by holding down the CONTROL key and pressing the C key, your problem should be solved. This 'command' returns the user to the prompt line, and should cancel the current command. **CONTROL C** can also be used to exit from the menu bar.

❏ Summary

1. OSNAP can be used to reference points on existing entities, and aids the drawing of new entities.
2. An *OSNAP mode* can be preset by the user to always give a desired OSNAP qualifier. Suppose that we want to set OSNAP to ENDpoint, then at the command prompt line

    enter   OSNAP<R>
    AutoCAD prompts   Object snap modes
    enter   END <R>.

    This means that you will not need to select ****ENDpoint from the menu.
3. You can 'over-ride' the above qualifier by selecting another OSNAP mode from the '****' list.
4. To cancel the preset mode, enter **OSNAP** then **<RETURN>**.

Activity

Attempt Tutorial 4, which consists of lines and circles. The use of OSNAP will be needed to obtain certain points, e.g. the circle centres, etc.

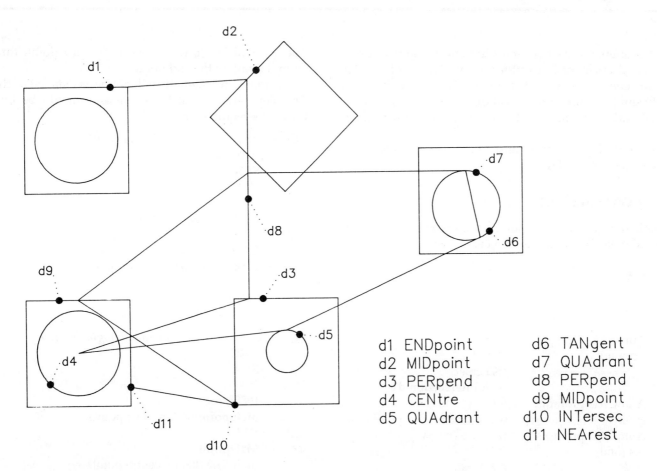

Fig. 13.1. OSNAP with LINE command.

14. Arc creation

AutoCAD offers the user several different methods of drawing arcs, and these methods utilise combinations of arc start point, arc end point, included angle, etc. All methods are basically similar in use and we will draw five arcs by different methods, and leave the user to investigate the others themselves.

Use the drawing **A:DRG1** consisting of the squares, circles and so on, and refer to Fig. 14.1.

Three point method

This method requires a start point, an intermediate point and an end point on the arc circumference, so select

>   **DRAW**
>   **ARC**
>   **3 POINT**

1. AutoCAD prompts respond

   ```
   Start point
   ****
   ```
   INTersec
   pick intersection d1

2. AutoCAD prompts enter

   ```
   Second point
   @-20,10<R>   (i.e. point d2).
   ```

3. AutoCAD prompts respond

   ```
   End point
   ****
   ```
   NEArest
   pick line d3

The arc will be drawn in from the start point, through the second point, to the end point.

The following methods will not be as detailed as that above. The steps (1)–(3) will be given, and should be followed to create the required arc.

SCE – start, centre and end point method

>   **ARC**
>   **SCE**

1. ****
   MIDpoint
   pick line d4 (arc start point)

2. ****
   CENtre
   pick circle d5 (arc centre point)

3. ****
   MIDpoint
   pick line d6 (arc end point).

SCA – start, centre and included angle method

>   **ARC**
>   **SCA**

1. ****
   INTersec
   pick point d7 (arc start point)

2. ****
   MIDpoint
   pick line d8 (arc centre point)

3. **120** from keyboard (arc included angle).

32 *Beginning AutoCAD*

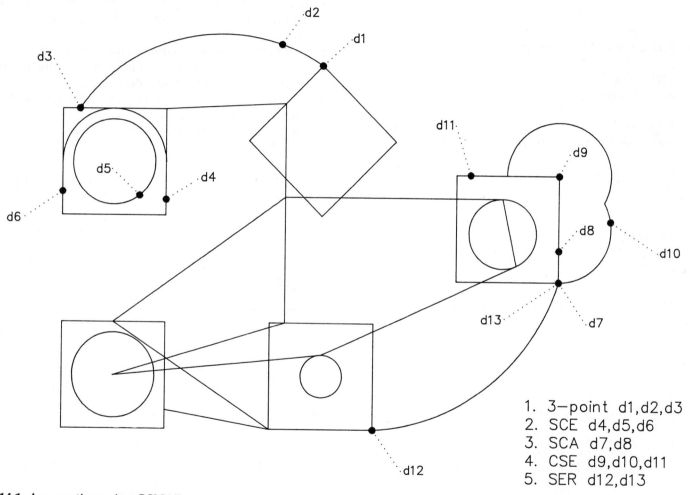

Fig. 14.1. Arc creation using OSNAP.

1. 3-point d1,d2,d3
2. SCE d4,d5,d6
3. SCA d7,d8
4. CSE d9,d10,d11
5. SER d12,d13

CSE – centre, start and end point method

        ARC
        CSE
1.   ****
        INTersec
        pick point d9 (arc centre point)
2.   ****
        ENDpoint
        pick arc d10 (arc start point)
3.   ****
        NEArest
        pick line d11 (arc end point).

SER – start, end point and radius method

        ARC
        SER
1.   ****
        INTersec
        pick point d12 (arc start point)
2.   ****
        INTersec
        pick point d13 (arc end point)
3.   100 from keyboard (arc radius).

Your drawing should now resemble Fig. 14.1. Save As... **A:DRG1**.

❏ Summary

1. The ARC method selected will always depend on how the arc is to be drawn, and on the 'information' available.
2. use of OSNAP is essential when drawing arcs.
3. Arcs are normally drawn anti-clockwise, although this can be altered to clockwise if desired.
4. Arcs may be drawn the 'wrong way' if the start and end points are selected in the wrong order.
5. The abbreviations for the arc commands are

    S – arc start point   C – arc centre point
    E – arc end point   A – arc 'included' angle
    L – arc length   R – arc radius.
    D – arc diameter

Activity

Attempt Tutorial 5, which consists of different arc drawings.

15. Fillet and chamfer

Use the **File, Open...** option with **A:WORKDRG** and refer to Fig. 15.1 on page 36. We will now add the fillet radii and chamfers.

Fillet

In AutoCAD a fillet is an EDIT function as it is altering entities which have already been drawn. Thus FILLET is found in the EDIT menu, so select from the screen menu

EDIT
next
FILLET
Radius

AutoCAD prompts	Enter fillet radius
enter	**20<R>**
AutoCAD prompts	Select first object
respond	**pick line d1**.
AutoCAD prompts	Select second object
respond	**pick line d2**.

The fillet radius will be drawn in, and the 'corner lines' will be erased. Now add the other two fillets using the radii values given.

Chamfer

Chamfer is also an EDIT function, and the selection sequence is

EDIT
CHAMFER
Distance.

AutoCAD prompts	Enter first chamfer distance
enter	**25<R>**
AutoCAD prompts	Enter second chamfer distance
enter	**25<R>**
AutoCAD prompts	Select first line
respond	**by picking line d3**.
AutoCAD prompts	Select second line
respond	**by picking line d4**.

Like the fillet, the chamfer will be drawn in and the 'corners' will be erased. Now add the other two chamfers, which require two different distances.

Before leaving this drawing try the following

Fillet and chamfer

1. Draw any two inclined lines near to each other, but not touching. Select **FILLET** then **Radius 0** and pick the two lines. The command should extend both lines until they meet. The same effect is obtained with **CHAMFER Distance 0**.
2. Draw two circles, not touching and select **FILLET Radius** and enter a value for the radius. Pick the two circles and a 'filleted' arc should be drawn between them.
3. Draw two intersecting circles, and repeat the FILLET command, selecting the circles. Note the effect.

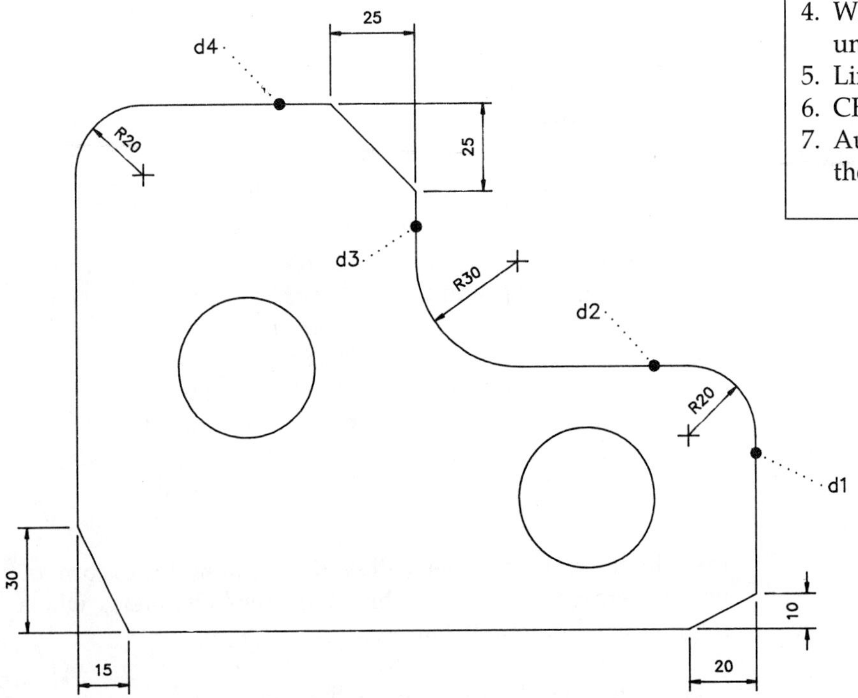

Now ERASE all extra lines and circles and save your edited drawing as **A:WORKDRG**.

❑ Summary

1. FILLET and CHAMFER are both EDIT commands.
2. FILLET requires a radius before it can be used.
3. With FILLET, radius 0 will extend two entities until they meet.
4. When a radius has been entered, it becomes the default until a new value is entered.
5. Lines, circles and arcs can be filleted.
6. CHAMFER requires two distances to be entered.
7. AutoCAD will assume the second chamfer distance is the same as the first, unless a different value is entered.

Fig. 15.1.

16. Offset, change and LTSCALE

We will now add centre lines to the A:WORKDRG drawing which was saved after the fillet and chamfer exercise, so **Open...** the drawing file **A:WORKDRG** and refer to Fig. 16.1 on the next page.

Offset

Select from the screen menu

    DRAW
    OFFSET

AutoCAD prompts	Offset distance or through
enter	**50<R>**
AutoCAD prompts	Select objects to offset
respond	**by picking line d1**.
AutoCAD prompts	Side to offset?
respond	**by picking a point d2** any where to the right of the line d1.

The vertical line selected will be offset a distance of 50 to the right and will pass through the circle centre point. OFFSET will copy the target entity **PARALLEL** to itself by the amount entered by the user.

Now use the command to OFFSET the other three lines using the offset values given in the figure.

Change

The four lines that have been offset are all continuous and not centre lines as we would like. This is because we *offset a continuous line*. To alter the appearance of these lines, we will use the CHANGE command, so select

    EDIT
    CHANGE.

AutoCAD prompts	Select objects
respond	**by picking the four offset lines** then **<RETURN>**.
AutoCAD prompts	Properties
respond	**LType** from menu
	centre from menu
	<RETURN> to end sequence.

The lines will have been changed to centre lines, although their appearance may not be as required.

LTSCALE

Select from the screen menu
> **AutoCAD**
> **SETTINGS**
> **next**
> **LTSCALE**

AutoCAD prompts   `New scale factor <1>`
enter   **0.5<R>**

Your four offset lines should now resemble centre lines in appearance. Now save your drawing.

❑ *Summary*

1. OFFSET can be found in the DRAW and EDIT menus.
2. Lines, circles and arcs can all be offset.
3. The entity selected to be offset, is offset in linetype and colour.
4. Using the puck RETURN button to recall the last command is very useful with OFFSET.
5. CHANGE is a very powerful command and can be used to alter the linetype, colour and layer of entities. It is also a very dangerous command to use as we will see later.
6. LTSCALE (linetype scale) is used to alter the appearance of entities. An LTSCALE value of 0.5 is reasonable for A3 paper.
7. The LTSCALE can be activated by entering LTSCALE at the prompt line. This is quicker than using the menu selection?

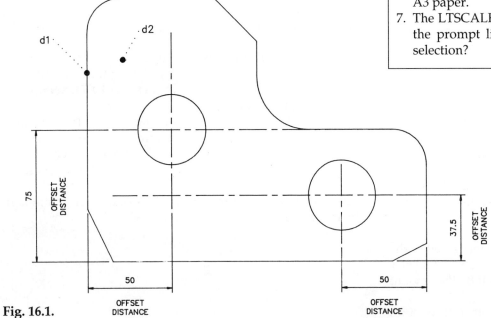

Fig. 16.1.

17. User exercise 2

Open the drawing file **A:DRG1** and erase all entities except those shown in part (a) of Fig. 17.1 shown below. Now use the OFFSET and CHANGE commands to produce part (b). There is no need to save this modified drawing.

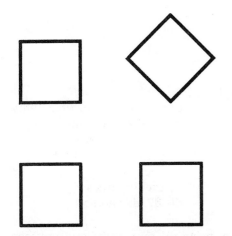

(a) Entities from A:DRG1 which have to be kept.

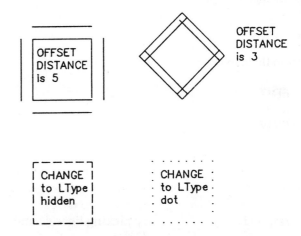

(b) Using OFFSET and CHANGE.

Fig. 17.1.

18. Extend and trim

These two commands are used extensively with drawings, and with the OFFSET command give three of the most useful commands in the AutoCAD package. The user should become proficient in their use.

Open the file **A:WORKDRG** and refer to Fig. 18.1. We will alter the length of the centre lines to give an 'even appearance' through the two circles.

Extend

Select from the menu

> **EDIT**
> **next**
> **EXTEND.**

AutoCAD prompts	Select boundary edge(s) (i.e. what entity do you want to extend up to) select objects
respond	**by picking lines d1 and d3<R>.**
AutoCAD prompts	Select objects to extend
respond	**by picking lines d2 and d4<R>.**

Now extend the other centre lines as shown in Fig. 18.1(b).

Offset

Use the OFFSET command to offset the two circles 5 mm 'outwards', as shown in Fig. 18.1(c).

Trim

Select from the menu

> **EDIT**
> **next**
> **TRIM**

AutoCAD prompts	Select cutting edge(s)... (i.e. what entity do you want to trim up to Select objects
respond	**by picking circle d5<R>.**
AutoCAD prompts	Select objects to trim
respond	**by picking lines d6, d7, d8, d9<R>.**

Now TRIM the other lines using the same technique and then ERASE the two offset circles. Your drawing should now resemble Fig. 18.1(d) with the circle centre lines having a better appearance.

Save the drawing as **A:WORKDRG** for future work.

❏ Summary

1. EXTEND and TRIM complement one another, and both are EDIT commands.
2. Both have the same format: select the boundary to extend up to, or trim up to and select the objects to extend or trim.
3. Most entities can be extended or trimmed.

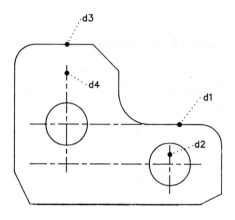

a) ORIGINAL with points for EXTEND.

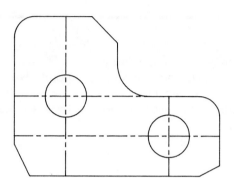

b) Effect of EXTEND command.

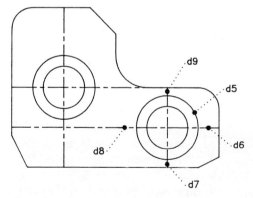

c) OFFSET circles and points for TRIM command.

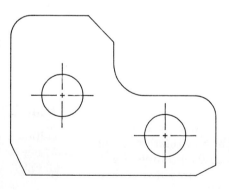

d) Effect of TRIM command.

Fig. 18.1. EXTEND and TRIM commands.

19. Simple text

It is always useful to add text to drawings. This may simply be a name and date, but could also be a parts listing or a company title block, etc. While text will be dealt with in greater detail later, it is considered worthwhile for the user to add simple text to all drawings from now on.

Text is a DRAW command, the sequence being

DRAW
next
TEXT

The user is now faced with a sub-menu of

align
centre
fit
middle
right

By picking any point on the screen as the **start point** for the text, the user then enters the **text height and rotation angle** as numbers from the keyboard in reply to the prompts, e.g. 5 for the height and 0 for the angle. The required text is then typed in from the keyboard and **<RETURN>** pressed when finished. The text will then be inserted at the selected point.

Selecting **centre**, then picking a point on the screen, results in the typed text being centred about the selected point. The height and angle prompts appear to the user.

Fit will allow text to be fitted in between two selected points. No prompts are asked.

Figure 19.1 below illustrates these effects, and at present these are considered adequate for the user.

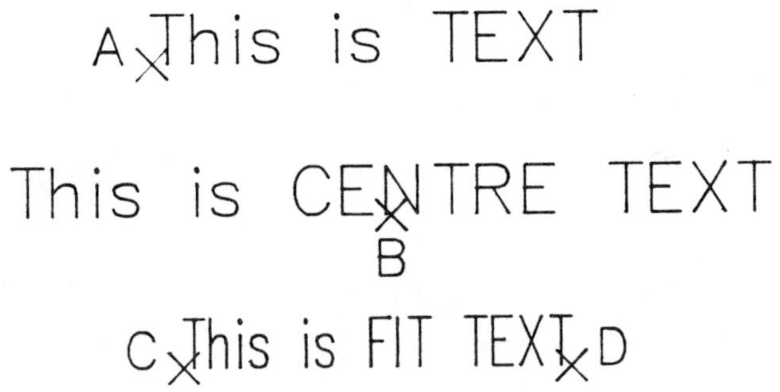

A×This is TEXT

This is CE×NTRE TEXT
B

C×This is FIT TEXT×D

Fig. 19.1.

Activity

Tutorials 6–8 will allow the user to try the commands which have been discussed up until now. Make use of the OFFSET, CHANGE and TRIM commands as well as the other commands. The drawings all consist of lines, circles, arcs and text. Co-ordinate input will be required. Do not worry if you cannot get the drawings exactly as shown. I may have sneaked in one or two commands not yet known to you.

20. Dimensioning

AutoCAD has *automatic dimensioning*. This means that the user does not become involved with measuring, and simply selects the entity to be dimensioned. AutoCAD does the calculations and displays the actual dimension as well as the proper dimension line to British Standards.

The Release 12 dimension capabilities are different from earlier versions. The same commands are there, but Release 12 has an addition to the menu bar which allows selection of all the dimension commands. The on-screen and the pull-down dimension menus are shown in detail in Fig. 20.1(a).

The basic dimension types are shown in Fig. 20.1(b) and are

- linear which may be (a) of individual lines, (b) using the baseline concept or (c) using the continue concept
- diameter of circles
- radius of circles and arcs
- angular dimensions between lines
- leader which takes the dimension 'outside' the entity.

To demonstrate dimensioning we will use the drawing file **A:WORKDRG** so open this file.

Linear dimensioning

With this exercise we will dimension using the on-screen menu and leave the user to investigate the menu bar selection, so refer to Fig. 20.2 and select from the menu

AutoCAD
DIM:
Horizontl

AutoCAD prompts	First extension line origin
respond with	****ENDpoint and pick line d1.
AutoCAD prompts	Second extension line origin
respond with	****INTersec and pick point d2.
AutoCAD prompts	Dimension line location
respond with	**picking any point d3** above the line being measured
AutoCAD prompts	Dimension text <100.00>
respond with	**<RETURN>**

The dimension should be inserted above the line with a value of 100.00. All of this dimension (i.e. the extension lines and the arrows) is a single entity, and would be erased by a single ERASE command.

You should still be in the **Dim: mode** at the command prompt line, so select from the screen menu

a) From Root Menu ie DIM:
   Aligned
   Angular(*)
   Diameter(*)
   Horizontl(*)
   Leader(*)
   Ordinate
   Radius(*)
   Rotated
   Vertical(*)
   Edit
   DimStyle
   Dimvars(*)
   next-------->   Baseline(*)
   Exit   Continue(*)
                    Centre(*)
                    Status

Items marked (*) are those which will be discussed.

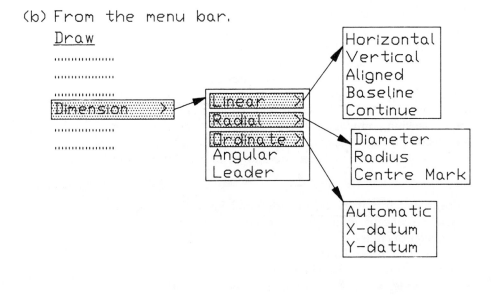

Fig. 20.1(a). The dimension menu.

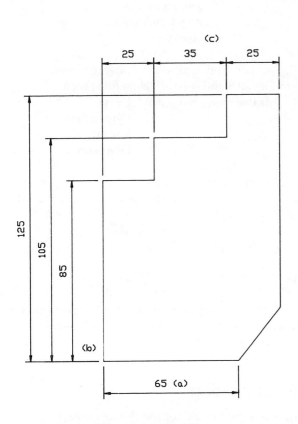

Fig. 20.1(b). Basic dimensions.

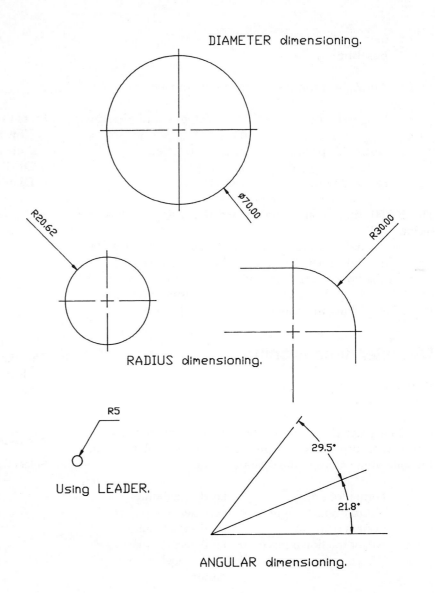

Dimensioning 45

next	
Baseline	
AutoCAD prompts	`Second extension line origin`
Respond with	****ENDpoint and pick line d4.**
AutoCAD prompts	`Dimension text <200.00>`
respond with	**<RETURN>**

The 200.00 dimension should be inserted using the baseline technique.

Now try and add the other dimensions shown in Fig. 20.2. The right-hand dimensions are vertical using **baseline**, while those at the bottom are horizontal using **continuous**. Use the OSNAP and reference existing entities using END and/or INT when picking the dimension extension line origins.

Diameter dimensioning

Before proceeding with this topic, we will reset the number of decimal places of the dimensions to 0. To do this make sure you have the command prompt empty (CONTROL C if not), and then enter the word **UNITS** at the command line. The screen will turn black and prompts will be displayed. Enter the following values to the various prompts

Format of units	2	i.e. decimal units
No. of digits to right	0	i.e. 0 decimal places
System of angles	1	i.e. decimal angles
No. of fractional places	0	i.e. 0 decimal places
Direction for angle	0	i.e. 3 o'clock is angle datum
Clockwise?	N	i.e. positive angles are anti-clockwise negative angles are clockwise.

Press **F1** to 'flip' screen from text to the drawing screen. Now refer to Fig. 20.3 and *erase all centre lines*, then

AutoCAD	or use menu bar with **Draw**
DIM	**Dimensions >**
Diameter	**Radial >**
	Diameter.

AutoCAD prompts	`Select arc or circle`
select	**pick a point on the circle d5**
AutoCAD prompts	`Dimension text <40>`
select	**<RETURN>**
AutoCAD prompts	`Enter leader length for text`
select	**<RETURN>**

The diameter dimension will be positioned at the point on the circle which was picked, the diameter symbol will be displayed and centre lines will be added.

Radius dimensioning

Select from the on-screen menu (or use the menu bar)

DIM:
Radius

AutoCAD prompts	`Select arc or circle`
select	****NEArest, and pick a point d6 on the circle**

46 *Beginning AutoCAD*

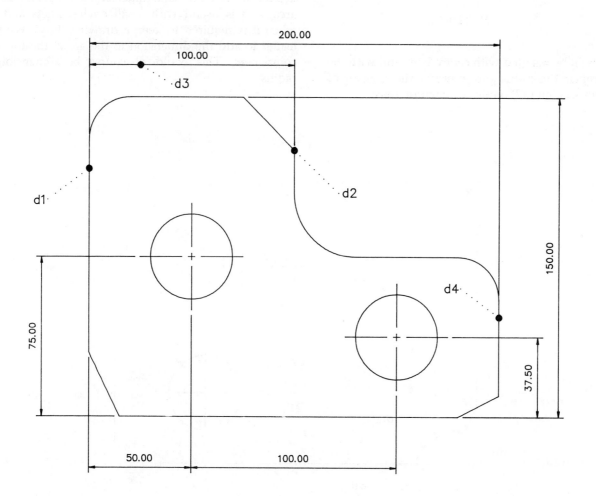

Fig. 20.2.

Dimensioning 47

AutoCAD prompts	Dimension text <20>
select	**<RETURN>**
AutoCAD prompts	Enter leader length for text
select	**<RETURN>**

The dimension will be inserted with centre lines and with the R20 text. Now repeat this radius procedure for the large arc of radius 30, picking a point (d7) on the arc circumference.

Leader dimensioning

Leaders are used to 'take dimension text outside' the drawing area, and is useful with small circles, fillets and generally when it is required to keep a drawing 'tidy'. We will use a leader to add the dimension to the arc at the top left of the component. This could of course be dimensioned using radius.

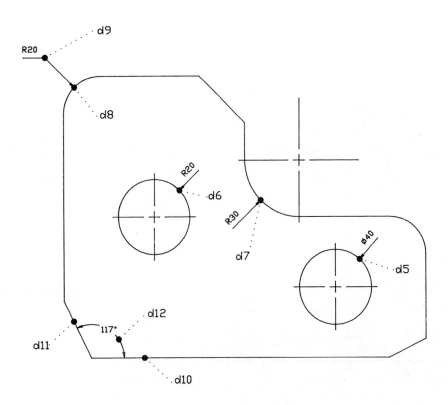

Fig. 20.3.

48   *Beginning AutoCAD*

Select from the screen menu

DIM:
Leader

AutoCAD prompts	`Leader start`
select	****NEArest and pick a point d8 on the arc**
AutoCAD prompts	`To point`
select	**point d9 outside the arc** then **<RETURN>**
AutoCAD prompts	`Dimension text <?>`
enter	**R20** then **<RETURN>**.

Angular dimensioning

AutoCAD allows angular dimensioning between two lines, so select

DIM:
Angular

AutoCAD prompts	`Select arc, circle, line or <RETURN>`
select	****NEArest and pick point d10 as shown.**
AutoCAD prompts	`Second point`
select	****NEArest and pick point d11 as shown.**
AutoCAD prompt	`Dimension arc location`
select	**pick a point similar to d12.**
AutoCAD prompts	`Dimension text <117>`
enter	**<RETURN>**

AutoCAD prompts	`Enter text location` and allows you to move the cursor and 'see' how the dimension arc and text will appear. Position to a suitable point then
enter	**<RETURN>**

Hopefully your drawing will be completely dimensioned as shown in Fig. 20.4. Dimensioning with AutoCAD is relatively simple, but it takes some practice to become familiar with the various selection procedures and the prompts. It is recommended that the user tries the various options by drawing a series of different lines, circles, etc. and adds different dimensions to these entities.

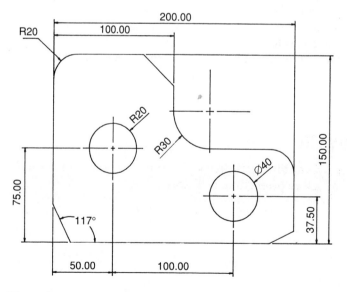

Fig.20.4.

Dimensioning 49

The default value

Any dimension that is selected has a **DEFAULT** value. This is the true value of the entity being dimensioned and appears as `<12.345>` and will be inserted into the dimension location. It is sometimes useful to **OVERRIDE** the default value to allow users to enter their own dimension value. This is especially true if you have set a large number of decimal places, e.g. 123.0000 and only want the 123 value to be entered as the dimension text. It is also true when using leaders when you want to enter R15, etc.

We will demonstrate the procedure by

(a) setting the UNITS to four decimal places
(b) drawing a horizontal line 123 units long
(c) selecting horizontal dimensions and selecting the two end points of the line
(d) the dimension text should be given as `<123.0000>`
(e) enter **123<R>**
(f) this value should be entered as the dimension text.

Activity

Draw some lines and circles of varying sizes and dimension them before proceeding to Tutorials 9–11.

❏ *Summary*

1. OSNAP is essential when dimensioning.
2. The diameter and degree symbols can be added to dimensions and text. This will be covered in a later section.
3. The default value can be over-ridden by the user entering their own dimension value from the keyboard.
4. Centre lines are inserted when dimensioning arcs and circles.
5. When arcs and circles are dimensioned, the dimension line starts at the point on the circle which is picked.
6. With small circles, leaders are best suited to entering the dimensions.
7. All dimensions have variables which include the size of the dimension arrows, the text size, the distance of the extension lines from the entity being dimensioned etc. These variables are controlled by the **DIMVARS** (dimension variables) and is really beyond the scope of this book, although we will discuss them in a later chapter.
8. The options available with the dimension command are extensive and not all have been investigated. I will leave the reader to investigate the dimension menu. Those dimensions discussed in this chapter are sufficient for normal drawings.
9. To leave the DIM menu, select **Exit** from the screen.

21. Display and view

These menu items are found in the on-screen menu (**DISPLAY**) and the menu bar (**View**) and basically give the same options. The commands which interest us at this stage of our learning process are

DISPLAY	View
PAN:	Redraw
REDRAW:	Zoom >
REGEN:	Pan
ZOOM:	

PAN: moves the drawing screen linearly by an amount determined by the user, i.e. by picking a start point and a displacement. It can sometimes lead to drawings 'disappearing' from the screen.
REDRAW: this command will probably have been used by now. It is a useful command after having erased entities from your drawings as it 'tidies up' the blips and so on.
REGEN: similar to REDRAW and is useful in giving arcs and circles a better definition.
ZOOM: probably one of the most commonly used AutoCAD commands. It allows the user to enlarge areas of the drawing screen for more detailed work, and should be used at all possible opportunities. The command has its own sub-menu, of which the most commonly used options are

ZOOM All – does what it says, giving all entities which have been drawn on the screen. It is especially useful in finding out if entities have been drawn 'outside the display'
ZOOM Previous – returns to the previous screen, if one exists
ZOOM Window – the most useful option, as it allows the user to window an area of the drawing for enlargement, i.e. it magnifies an area of the screen.

There are other ZOOM options, but I would not recommend these at present, especially *not* the ZOOM Dynamic option.

Note
I personally find that using the screen menu or pull-down menu for these commands tedious. It is just as simple to enter them at the command prompt line, for example

(a) if you want to redraw, enter **REDRAW** then <R>
(b) if you want to zoom a window, enter **ZOOM<R>**, then **w<R>**
(c) similarly to zoom all, enter **ZOOM<R>** then **a<R>**
(d) remember when entering from the keyboard, the word can be in upper or lower case, i.e. 'zoom' or 'ZOOM'.

22. Editing: copy, move, rotate, mirror

AutoCAD has many useful EDIT commands, four of which will be demonstrated in this chapter. Load AutoCAD and from the menu bar, select **Files** then **Open...** with the drawing name **A:WORKDRG**. Now *erase all entities* to leave the diagram as shown in Fig. 22.1 and then ZOOM All.

Copy

Select from the screen menu

    EDIT
    COPY

AutoCAD prompts respond with	Select objects (a) enter 'w' then <R> for window or (b) **pick Select Objects then Window**.
AutoCAD prompts respond	First corner **pick point d1**.
AutoCAD prompts respond	Other corner **pick point d2**.
AutoCAD prompts	9 found (note: only complete entites are highlighted) Select Objects
respond	**pick Select Objects then Add**.
AutoCAD prompts respond	Select Objects **pick d3, d4, d5, d6 and d7 then <R>**.
AutoCAD prompts	Base point or displacement
respond	****INTersec and pick point d8**.

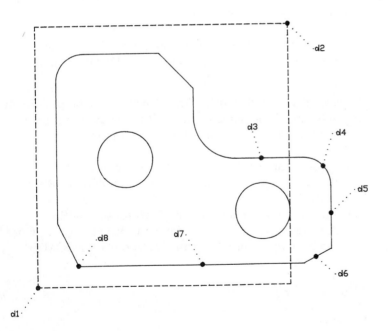

Fig. 22.1.

AutoCAD prompts	Second point of displacement	respond		Select Objects from screen menu.
enter	400,50<R>		Remove Select Objects Crossing	

Your drawing should now resemble Fig. 22.2 and you are starting to get worried because part of the drawing is off the screen. This can happen when using certain commands, e.g. COPY, MOVE, PAN, etc. However, all is not lost.

At the command prompt line, enter **ZOOM** then **A** and your drawing with the copy effect should fill the screen as Fig. 22.3.

Move

Now refer to Fig. 22.3, and select

    EDIT
    next
    MOVE
    Select Objects
    Crossing

AutoCAD prompts respond	First point **by picking a point d1**.
AutoCAD prompts respond	Other point **and pick a point d2** (note the highlight effect).
AutoCAD prompts respond	Select objects **Select Objects then Add from screen menu.**
AutoCAD prompts respond	Select objects **by picking d3, d4, d5** then
AutoCAD prompts	Select objects

AutoCAD prompts	Select objects
respond	**pick points d6 and d7** then <RETURN> (to end the selection sequence).
AutoCAD prompts	Base point or displacement
respond	****INTersec and pick point d8.**
AutoCAD prompts	Second point of displacement
enter	**330,320** then **<RETURN>** to complete the command.

Your drawing should now resemble Fig. 22.4, one of the circles having been 'left behind' with the MOVE command.

Rotate

Using Fig. 22.4, select

    EDIT
    next
    ROTATE
    Select Objects
    Previous

AutoCAD prompts respond	Select objects **<RETURN>** and note 'moved shape' highlighted.
AutoCAD prompts	Select objects

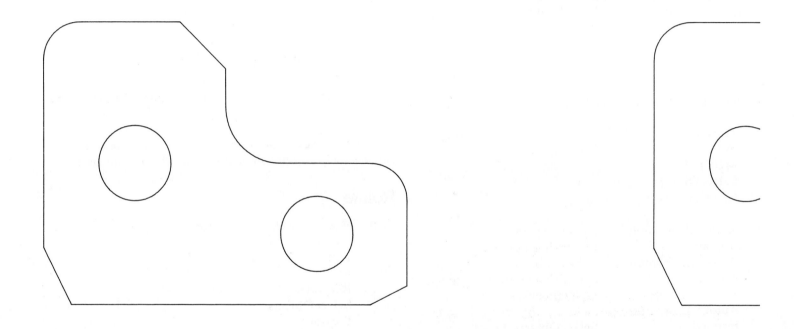

Fig. 22.2. WORKDRG after COPY command.

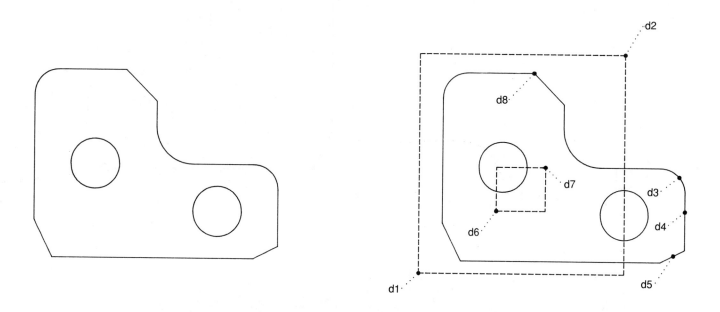

Fig. 22.3. WORKDRG after ZOOM All, with points for the MOVE command.

Editing: copy, move, rotate, mirror

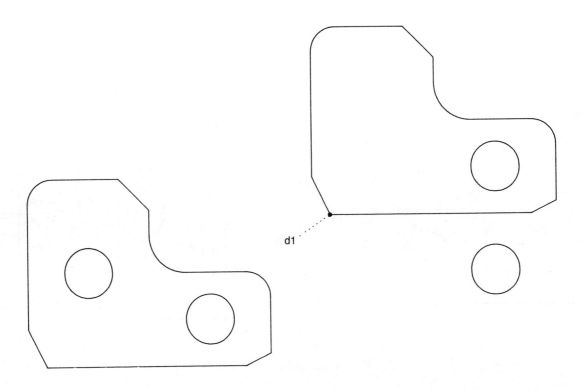

Fig. 22.4. WORKDRG after the MOVE command, with point for ROTATE command.

respond	**Select Objects Remove**.
AutoCAD prompts	`Select objects`
respond	**pick the circle inside the shape** **<RETURN>**
AutoCAD prompts	`Base point`
respond	****INTersec and pick point d1**.
AutoCAD prompts	`Rotation angle`
enter	**30 then <RETURN>**

Your final drawing should now resemble Fig. 22.5. Save it if you want using another name.

Mirror

Begin a new drawing and refer to Fig. 22.6. Draw the shape given and then select

EDIT
next
MIRROR
Select Objects
Window and 'window' the complete shape

AutoCAD prompts	`First point on mirror line`
respond	****INTersec and pick point d1**.
AutoCAD prompts	`Second point on mirror line`
respond	****INTersec and pick point d2**.
AutoCAD prompts	`Delete old objects <N>`
respond	**<RETURN>**, i.e. accept the *no* default.

The shape will then be mirrored about the right vertical line.

Now ERASE the three vertical lines in the middle and **REDRAW**. Have three vertical lines appeared? *Work this out for yourself.*

The selection set

By now users should be familiar with the selection set. This is the name given to the 'Select Objects' option in the EDIT commands, e.g. Window, Crossing, etc. Four new options have been added to Release 12, these being

ALL – selects all entities in the drawing which are not on locked layers.
FENCE – selects all entities in the drawing that are crossed by a fence defined by the user.
CPOLYGON – selects all entities within or touching a polygon made by the user.
CWINDOW – as CPOLYGON, but only entities completely enclosed in the defined polygon.

Refer to Fig. 22.7(a) and (b) and try these options.

Activity

Attempt Tutorials 12–14 which use the commands in this chapter, then as a bit of light relief try Tutorials 15 and 16.

Editing: copy, move, rotate, mirror

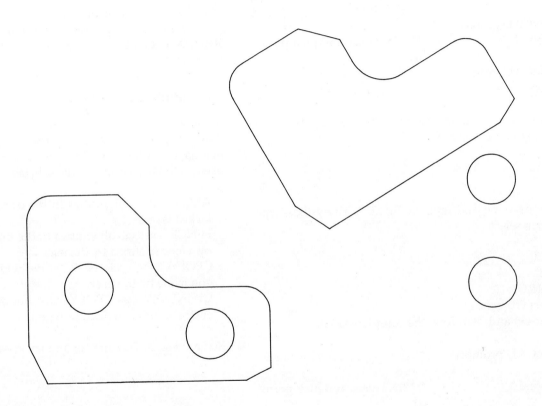

Fig. 22.5. WORKDRG after ROTATE command.

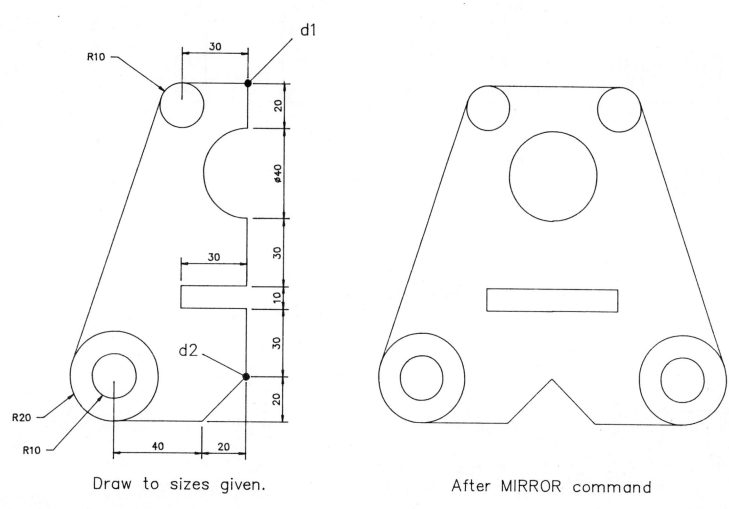

Fig. 22.6. Drawing for MIRROR command.

Editing: *copy, move, rotate, mirror*

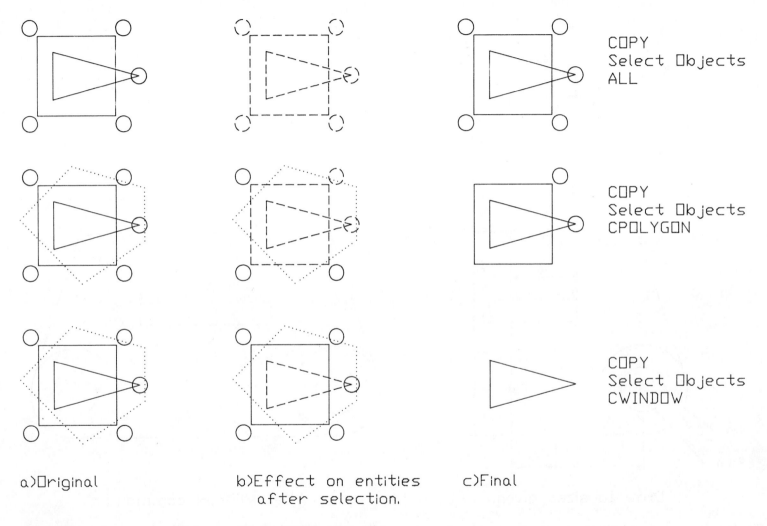

Fig. 22.7(a). Selection set additions, using the COPY command.

60 *Beginning AutoCAD*

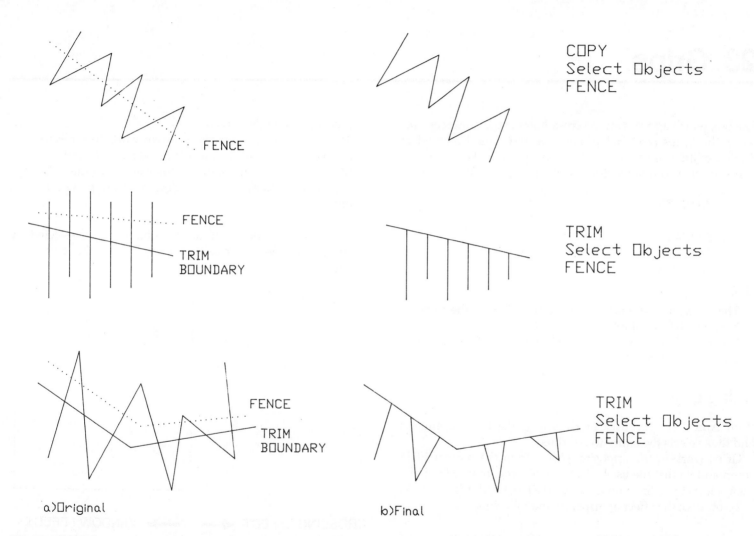

Fig. 22.7(b). Selection set additions, using COPY and TRIM.

Editing: copy, move, rotate, mirror 61

23. Grips

The box which appears on the cross-hairs of the on-screen cursor is the 'grips box' and provides a very useful method of limited editing of entities without using the EDIT command. There are five editing facilities available with GRIPS

    STRETCH
    MOVE
    ROTATE
    SCALE
    MIRROR.

Note
1. The grips box should not be confused with the OSNAP box, which has a similar appearance.
2. When a DRAW command is selected, e.g. LINE, the grips box will disappear from the cross-hairs.

Using grips

With AutoCAD, the user firstly selects the EDIT command and then selects the entity to be edited.

Grips work in the opposite 'sense' from the normal EDIT command, in that the user selects the object(s) to be edited and then selects the edit command, i.e. STRETCH,.MOVE....

To observe the effect of grips, try the following

1. Select an area on the screen which has nothing drawn and move the on-screen cursor to this area.
2. Pick a point on the screen.
3. Move the cursor upwards or downwards to the right and observe that a 'solid window type box' is obtained.
4. Move the cursor upwards or downwards to the left of the pick point and note that a 'dotted crossing type box' is obtained.

Using the grip box thus allows objects to be selected by either a window or crossing effect, before the editing is applied. See Fig. 23.1.

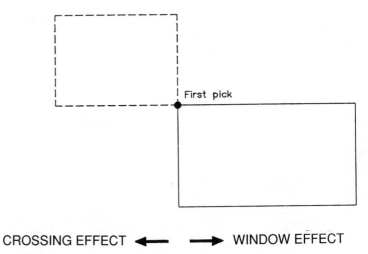

CROSSING EFFECT ⟵   ⟶ **WINDOW EFFECT**

Fig. 23.1.

62 *Beginning AutoCAD*

How grips work

Grips allow limited editing but at a faster speed. When the gripmode is on and when an entity is selected, a 'blue' box will appear at the OSNAP points, i.e. at endpoint and midpoint for lines, and at centre and quadrant for circles, etc. There are three different types of grip (see Fig. 23.2)

- Cold grips: appear on the selected entity in blue, but the entity is not highlighted. Such an entity cannot be edited using grips but it can be snapped to.
- Warm grips: appear in blue on highlighted entities. These have a dashed effect and will be affected by grip editing.
- Hot grips: appear as a solid (red) box when the grip is picked, and will act as a base for the grip editing options.

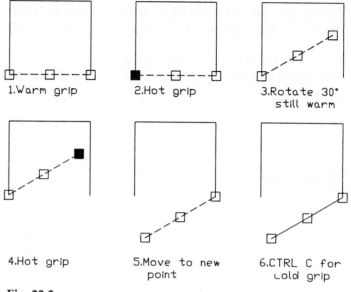

Fig. 23.3.

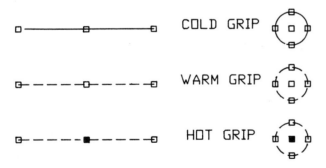

Fig. 23.2.

Now draw a square on the screen and refer to Fig. 23.3.

1. Use the cursor to pick the bottom line of the square. It will change appearance and blue grip boxes will appear at the OSNAP points. This is a warm grip.
2. Pick the left hand grip box. It will turn red indicating that we now have a hot grip.
3.   AutoCAD prompts   `**STRETCH**`
                                                               `<Stretch point>...`
       enter   **\<RETURN\>**.
       AutoCAD prompts   `**MOVE**`
                                                                `<Move to point>...`
       enter   **\<RETURN\>**.
       AutoCAD prompts   `**ROTATE**`
                                                                 `<Rotation angle>...`
       enter   **30\<R\>**

The line will be rotated through 30°, and will still appear as a warm grip.

4. Pick the grip box at the other end of the line to make it hot.
5. Select the MOVE option, and move to the endpoint as indicated.
6. Enter CONTROL C to make a cold grip.
7. Continue with grips or end the sequence with CONTROL C.

❏ Summary

1. Grips allow quick limited editing without using the EDIT command.
2. Grips *do not have to be used for editing*. The EDIT–MOVE command is still perfectly valid as are ROTATE, MIRROR, etc. Grips allow an additional facility for the user.
3. Grips work by (a) selecting the entity or (b) selecting the command. This is the opposite of the normal AutoCAD commands.
4. The grip box can sometimes prove rather irritating to the user. If you are editing an entity and do not select it correctly, then the grip window will appear. Do avoid this, it is possible to turn the grip box off. This is achieved with the following sequence

enter	*AutoCAD prompts*	*enter*
GRIPS	New value for GRIPS<1>	0<R>
PICKFIRST	New value for PICKFIRST<1>	0<R>

If you are not going to use grips, then I recommend that you turn the grip box off. It can be turned back on by entering 1 to the above commands.

24. Setting the drawing layout

Up until now, all drawings have been done without any attempt at an organised layout. AutoCAD has the facility to allow the user a great deal of control over the drawing environment, for instance, size of text, size of paper, dimension style, name box and so on. For companies using AutoCAD this control is invaluable when it comes to details such as dimension arrow sizes, text style and printing.

Parameters can be **SET** every time a new drawing is started, but this is time consuming and errors may occur. It is preferable to have all standard requirements set automatically. This is achieved by making up a drawing called a *standard sheet*. It may also be called the *prototype drawing* or some other suitable name. Standard sheets should be made for each size of paper used. They should be A4, A3, A2, A1 and A0 standard sheets.

Each standard sheet should contain defaults for limits, mode settings, scales, units, dimension variables, which are appropriate to the company's normal daily requirements. Once these have been set, they will rarely be altered.

Making a standard sheet

We will assume that our requirements are for a standard A3 sheet, which we will call **STDA3**, so select from the menu bar, **Files** then **New...** and at the **New Drawing Name...** box enter **A:STDA3** and pick the **OK** box.

From the Root Menu select **SETTINGS**, and then select the following options, entering the values given below. Note that it may be necessary to re-select SETTINGS after each option.

Apertur	3
Pickbox	3
BLIPS	OFF
GRID	10
LIMITS	0,0 for lower left-hand
	420,297 for upper right-hand
LTSCALE	0.6
SNAP	10
UCSICON	OFF
UNITS	'system' – enter 2 for decimal units
	'digits' – enter 2 for decimal places
	'angle' – enter 1 for decimal angles
	'places' – enter 1 for decimal places
	'direction' – enter 0 for 3 o'clock position
	'cwise' – enter N to maintain anti-clockwise

F1 to return to graphics screen.

Now select **DRAW** then **LINE**, and draw lines

from 0,0
to 380,0
to 380,270
to 0,270
to close

then

ZOOM All

The rectangle drawn will allow an A3 drawing to be plotted full size if all entities are contained within it.

This is the basic standard A3 sheet. Other details may be added as required so save it as **A:STDA3**. What is being saved is an A3-sized piece of paper with a box drawn on it, but with certain variables set for future use.

25. Layers

So far all entities drawn have been of the CONTINUOUS linetype and only by using the CHANGE command has it been possible to obtain centre and hidden linetypes. This procedure for changing linetypes is rather inefficient and *is not recommended*. AutoCAD has a facility called **LAYERS** which allows the user to assign different linetypes and colours to different named layers. For example, a layer may be for *red continuous* lines, another may be for *green hidden* lines and yet another layer could be for *blue centre* lines. As well as linetypes and colours, layers can be used for specific drawing purposes – there may be a layer for dimensions only, one for hatching, one for construction lines and so on. Individual layers can be switched on or off as required by the user to mask out drawing entities which are not required.

The concept of layers can be imagined as a series of transparent overlays, each having its own linetype and colour. The overlay used for dimensions could be removed without affecting the rest of the drawing.

AutoCAD needs to draw entities on layers, hence a layer is available for the user when AutoCAD is loaded. This is **Layer 0** and has a *continuous* linetype with the colour **WHITE**. This is why all entities are drawn as full white lines (or black).

The layers which we will consider at present are

Usage	*Layer name*	*Layer colour*	*Layer line type*
Outlines	OUT	white	CONTINUOUS
Centre lines	CL	white	CENTRE
Hidden lines	HID	white	HIDDEN
Dimensions	DIM	white	CONTINUOUS
Text	TEXT	white	CONTINUOUS
Hatching	SECT	white	CONTINUOUS
Construction lines	CONS	red	CONTINUOUS

Notes

1. Before layers can be used they must be made by the user – the layer names, linetypes and colour must be entered.
2. AutoCAD allows new layers to be made by either (a) entering information at the command prompt line or (b) using the layer control dialogue box to enter information.
3. Layers are perhaps the most important concept in AutoCAD. They are *essential* for good and efficient draughting, and I will spend quite some time on them in this chapter. Readers *must* become proficient with layers, and if you find that you are not grasping the concept, then I suggest that you repeat the chapter. It may also be advisable to seek assistance from colleagues who understand layers.
4. Previous AutoCAD users will find that Release 12 has greatly improved the layer technique, and the dialogue boxes will prove an invaluable aid.
5. The dialogue box can be viewed from the menu bar, by selecting **Settings** then **Layer Control...**. The layout is as Fig. 25.1(a), and shows that layer 0 is current, has a linetype CONTINUOUS and is WHITE.

Study this dialogue box, noting the various names and

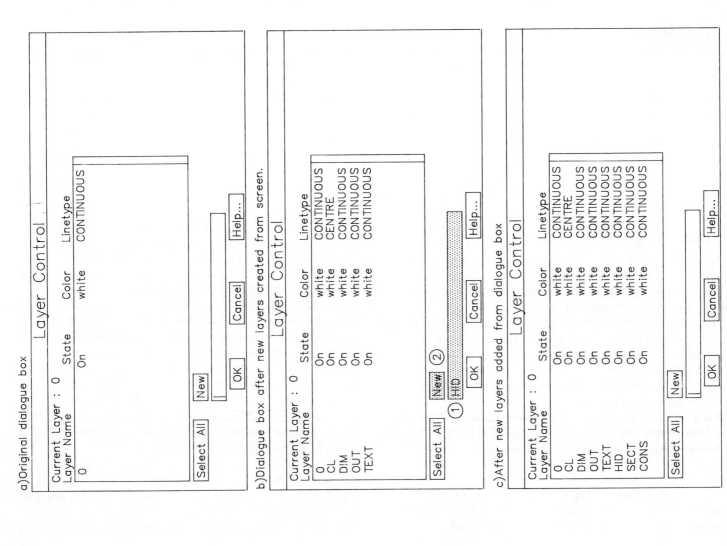

Fig. 25.1. Layer control. (a) Original dialogue box, (b) dialogue box after new layers created from screen, (c) after new layers added from dialogue box.

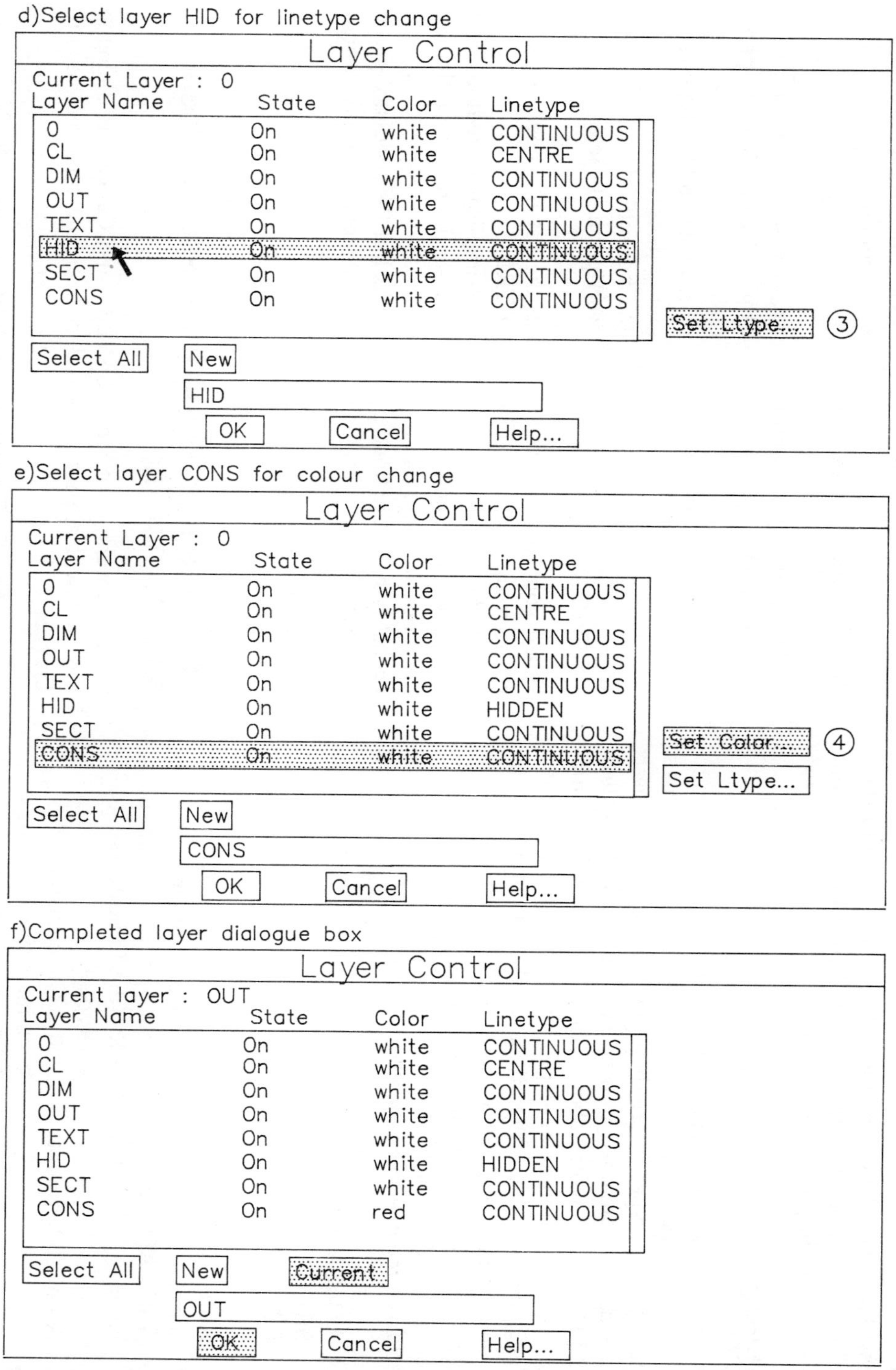

Fig. 25.1. Layer control. (d) Select layer HID for linetype change, (e) select layer CONS for colour change, (f) completed layer dialogue box.

that not all options are available at this instant. Available options are in bold type. Select the **Cancel** box when finished.
6. We will make the layers mentioned previously on our standard sheet, so open the drawing file A:STDA3 which contains your settings from the previous section.

Linetypes

Before proceeding with layers, it is necessary at this stage to talk about linetypes. AutoCAD Release 12 comes equipped with different linetypes (more than previous versions). These linetypes are all contained in a special AutoCAD file called **ACAD.LIN** – don't worry about this, it is background information. To use different linetypes, they must be *loaded into AutoCAD*, and users may already have all the linetypes available, while other users may not. I will assume that the ACAD.LIN file has not been loaded, and that the following sequence is required for all readers.

Select from the on-screen menu

    AutoCAD
    SETTINGS
    LINETYP

AutoCAD prompts	`?/Create/Load/Set`
select	**Load from the screen**.
AutoCAD prompts enter	`Linetype(s) to load` `*<R>` (this indicates *all* linetypes).
AutoCAD prompts	with a Dialogue box containing the following (a) `Pattern *.LIN` (b) `File ACAD`
select	**pick the OK box**.
AutoCAD prompts	by loading all the linetypes. If prompts occur at the command line, accept the `<Y>` default.

When all linetypes are loaded

AutoCAD prompts enter	`?/Create/Load/Set` **? then <RETURN> and pick OK**.
AutoCAD prompts	with a list of all linetypes, giving their names and a graphical description of each.

When you have browsed through the list of linetypes, then return to the drawing editor with **CTRL C**.

The above procedure may seem complicated, tedious and unnecessary to the reader, but it is essential to ensure that all linetypes are available to the user. Most existing systems will probably have the linetypes available, but the sequence given above is very useful to have available if some linetypes cannot be used.

Now that we have loaded the linetypes, we can now proceed to make our layers.

Layer creation using the on-screen menu and prompt line

Select from the Root Menu **LAYER...** and **Cancel** the dialogue box that will appear. Now select from the on-screen menu, **LAYER**

AutoCAD prompts	`?/Make/Set/New/ON/` `OFF/Color/Ltype/...` `Unlock`

70 *Beginning AutoCAD*

select	**pick New from screen**.	
AutoCAD prompts	`New layer name(s)`	
enter	**OUT,CL,TEXT,DIM<R>**	
AutoCAD prompts	`?/Make/Set...`	
select	**pick Ltype from screen**.	
AutoCAD prompts	`Linetype <CONTINUOUS>`	
enter	**<RETURN>** (i.e. accepting CONTINUOUS linetype)	
AutoCAD prompts	`Layer name(s) for linetype CONTINUOUS`	
enter	**OUT,TEXT,DIM<R>**	
AutoCAD prompts	`?/Make/Set...`	
select	**pick LTYPE from screen**.	
AutoCAD prompts	`Linetype <CONTINUOUS>`	
select	**pick centre from screen**.	
AutoCAD prompts	`Layer name(s) for linetype CENTRE`	
enter	**CL<R>**	
AutoCAD prompts	`?/Make/Set...`	
enter	**<RETURN>** to end this sequence.	

If you have completed this task properly, you have made four new layers. From the screen menu select **LAYER:** then **?**. The screen should turn to text mode and display the following

Layer name	State	Color	Linetype
0	On	7(white)	CONTINUOUS
CL	On	7(white)	CENTRE
DIM	On	7(white)	CONTINUOUS
OUT	On	7(white)	CONTINUOUS
TEXT	On	7(white)	CONTINUOUS

Current layer: 0
Prompt: `?/Make/Set...`

This should be the four layers that were entered in the sequence above. The layers are listed in alphabetical order, with their linetypes and colour. Only the CL layer had a different linetype, i.e. CENTRE, all others being CONTINUOUS. No colour was changed. Now **CTRL C** and **F1** to return to drawing mode.

Layer creation using the dialogue box

Select from the menu bar

> **Settings**
> **Layer Control...**

The dialogue box will appear as Fig.25.1(b), with the layers from the previous exercise displayed.

1. Enter **HID** at box 1 and pick **New** at box 2 – the HID layer will be added to the list of layers. Repeat this for the other new layers, i.e. SECT and CONS, adding the names and picking the New box. The dialogue box will then appear as Fig. 25.1(c).
2. Now select HID from the list of layers by placing the arrow over the name and **picking** it. The HID row will be highlighted in blue, and the name HID will appear in the layer name box as Fig. 25.1(d). Note that more options appear in bold text – they are available for selection. Select the **Set Ltype** box 3. The screen will display another pop-up dialogue box of the linetypes that were loaded from the earlier exercise. Use the arrow to select the *hidden* linetype then pick **OK**. Check that the linetype for the layer HID has been changed to HIDDEN. Select the **Clear All** box.
3. We are now going to change the colour of the CONS layer to red, so highlight and pick this layer form the list as Fig. 25.1(e). Now select the **Set Color** box 4. The screen will

Layers 71

now display the **Select Color** dialogue box with the range of colours available to the user. At this instance we will only consider the *nine standard colours* at the top of the screen. Move the arrow over the red square and 'pick it'. The name 'red' should be displayed in the color box with a red square beside it. Pick the OK box, and the Layer Control dialogue box will be returned with the CONS layer changed to red.
4. Before leaving the Layer Control dialogue box, we will make outline layer current, so move the arrow over the layer name OUT and pick it. The name OUT should appear in layer name box. Now pick the Current box, and OUT should appear opposite the Current Layer position at the top of the screen as Fig. 25.1(f).
5. If you are satisfied that all layers have been made as required, pick the OK box.
6. You will be returned to the drawing editor, and OUT should be displayed next to the Layer name in the Status line.

Note

Users may have noticed that there is a small coloured square in the status line to the left of the Layer name. This is an indication of the colour of the current layer, and in all instances up until now it has been black. It should still be black, as OUT is the current layer with a colour white (white gives black – confusing?). Recall the Layer Control... and make CONS the current layer if you can. When you return to the drawing screen, the box in the status line should be red. When you have achieved this, return the current layer to OUT.

Saving the standard sheet

Now that all our layers have been made, we want to save the standard sheet for future use, so select **Files** and **Save As...** and enter the drawing name as **A:STDA3**, i.e. we have added these layers to the settings made in the previous chapter. The standard sheet is thus a 'blank piece of paper' on which are settings to assist with our drawings as well as layers which have been made to our requirements. Thus this standard sheet has been made for A3 paper and the procedure for making layers should never be have to be repeated, although it may be necessary to add additional layers at a later time.

Using layers

Having made new layers, it is now possible to draw entities with hidden and centre linetypes simply by altering the **CURRENT** layer. The current layer has its name displayed at the left-hand end of the STATUS line. To modify or alter the current layer (note that I deliberately *do not* use the phrase CHANGE LAYERS, as this may cause the user to think of the **EDIT** command called **CHANGE**, and this is *not* the same concept) the **Layer Control...** dialogue box should be used. To make a layer current, simply use the pick arrow to highlight the line containing the layer name and then pick the Current box. The layer name will appear at the current layer position of the dialogue box, and when OK is selected, the layer name will then appear at the status line.

All future drawings should use the layer concept. If you are drawing outlines then OUT should be the current layer, if you are drawing centre lines then CL should be the current layer. Similarly DIM should be the current layer when dimensioning.

The Layer Control dialogue box also contains all the facilities to allow the user to switch layers on and off, freeze and thaw them and change the linetypes and colours. Probably the most common use of the dialogue box will be altering the current layer and turning layers on and off.

Using the standard sheet

From now on every drawing started will be a *new* drawing and will use the **A:STDA3** standard sheet, i.e. all drawings will have the layers and settings created for the standard sheet available and will not have to be reset.

The procedure when starting a new drawing will now be (1) select **Files** then **New...** and (2) at the New Drawing Name... box, enter

   A:NEWNAME=A:STDA3

This will load in A:STDA3 with all the settings and layers of the standard sheet, and when the drawing is complete the **Files** and **Save As...** option will result in the name NEWNAME appearing in the File box of the pop-up files dialogue box. Thus all the layers of the standard sheet are available to the user, but the A:STDA3 drawing is untouched, i.e. it is always be a 'blank piece of paper'.

Modifying layers

Earlier in the chapter, I stressed that the phrase **MODIFY LAYER** should be used and that CHANGE layer should not. These are two phrases which I have found confuses new (and experienced) AutoCAD users. Confusion does arise when using layers, and the fact that the CHANGE command has the word layer as an option in its sub-menu does not help.

CHANGE is an EDIT command and is used to alter the appearance of existing entities that have been drawn, for example

- an entity can have its linetype changed from continuous to centre (as has been achieved earlier)
- entities can have their colour changed with the command
- an entity can be 'moved' from one layer to another with CHANGE.

While the above are possible, they are not recommended. If the first option is used it could mean that two or three different linetypes are contained on the one layer. If a line is to be drawn as a hidden line or as a centre line, then the HID or CL layer should be made current and the line then drawn.

The CHANGE command *cannot be used to alter the current layer setting*. Layers can only be made current by (1) using the Layer Control dialogue box as described earlier and (2) using the SET option of the LAYER: command.

The new user to AutoCAD may be wondering why this section is long and laboured. Layers are the 'backbone' of AutoCAD, and without them the package would not be as useful or as powerful as it is. Layers give enormous benefits to the user and to companies who use AutoCAD. With layers, it is possible to have layers for special notes, calculations, costing, material used, etc. which would otherwise be on separate sheets of paper, i.e. all the data relating to a particular job can be kept on the one drawing file. By using the off option, the layers which apply only to the company will not then be 'seen' by unauthorised personnel.

Changing the prototype drawing name

The method described above for starting a new drawing (A:NEWNAME=A:STDA3) is perfectly valid, but there is another method which the user may wish to use. This is by changing the name of the prototype drawing. When the **New...** option is selected from the menu bar, the Create New Drawing dialogue box appears, with the prototype drawing name as **acad**. The user can alter this prototype drawing by

(a) double clicking onto the prototype name (acad)

(b) entering the standard sheet name, i.e. A:STDA3
(c) entering the required drawing name at the New Drawing Name box
(d) picking OK.

	existing	*required*
Prototype	acad	A:STDA3
New Drawing Name		A:MYDRG

Note there are two options available with the Create New Drawing dialogue box (1) no prototype and (2) retain as default.

If the second option is selected, it will mean that STDA3 is the prototype drawing for all future work. The user then enters the required new drawing name at the appropriate box, and the standard sheet is then 'called in' with all layers and settings 'set'.

My preference is to use the first method described. Entering A:NEWNAME=A:STDA3, but the two options are available.

Layer Locking

AutoCAD Release 12 has a new layer facility called LAYER LOCKING. This allows entities to remain visible but they cannot be edited. The benefit of layer locking is that entities which are on a locked layer can be referenced using OSNAP.

The complete list of layer options is

ON: all entities are shown and can be edited.
OFF: entities are not shown and therefore *will not* be edited.
FREEZE: similar to OFF but gives faster regeneration.
THAW: undoes a frozen layer.
LOCK: entities drawn are shown, but cannot be edited. However, they can be *referenced*.
UNLOCK : undoes a locked layer.

Care should be taken with layers which are OFF or FROZEN. If you are editing (e.g. MOVE, COPY) it may mean that you will not get the effect wanted. Think about it!

The Layer Control dialogue box gives the status of the various layers as follows

State	
On . . .	layer is ON
. . .	layer is OFF
On F .	layer is ON and FROZEN
On . L	layer is ON and LOCKED.

26. Adding text

Text was mentioned in a previous chapter but only very briefly to allow the user some extra drawing power. We will now discuss text in greater detail. Before proceeding, refer to Fig 26.1 and draw the basic shape as in part (a). Add the extra lines as in (b) and then use the EXTEND and TRIM commands to give the final shape as in (c). Use the **Save As...** option with the file name **A:EXER1** to save this shape, as it will be used in later exercises.

AutoCAD allows the user two different commands for the creation of text, although both produce exactly the same result. These commands are **TEXT** and **DTEXT** and are both DRAW commands. Both allow the user to add text entities to drawings using a variety of character patterns called **FONTS** (described later). The text can be entered with varying height and at different angles of rotation as well as with different justification.

Text

Using the shape created, refer to Fig. 26.2 and select

DRAW
next
TEXT.

AutoCAD prompts	`_TEXT Justify/Style/<Start Point>`
enter	**30,210** (the text start point).
AutoCAD prompts	`Height <?>`
enter	**10<R>**
AutoCAD prompts	`Rotation angle <0>`
enter	**0<R>** (i.e. text will be horizontal).
AutoCAD prompts	`Text:`
enter	**TEXT EXERCISE**

Note that nothing appears on the screen, although TEXT EXERCISE has been entered at the prompt line. When you press **<RETURN>** the text will be displayed on the screen at the selected start point.

To create multiple lines of text using this command requires the above sequence to be repeated every time.

DTEXT

The DTEXT (for DYNAMIC TEXT) is similar to the TEXT command, but it has two advantages in that (a) the user can 'see' the text as it is being entered from the keyboard and (b) it allows multiple lines of text to be entered at one 'pick'.

The prompts are the same as the TEXT prompts, so select

DRAW
DTEXT

and respond to the prompts with

200,210	text start point
6	height
0	rotation
your name	<R>
the date	<R>
<RETURN>	to end command.

Two lines of text should now appear at the selected start point, and you should have seen the text on the screen as it was being entered from the keyboard.

Now use the DTEXT command to add the rest of the text given in Fig. 26.2. The height is at your discretion, but bear in mind the appearance of the existing text, and the heights used.

Text justification

Text which is put on the screen can be positioned (*justified*) in different ways. AutoCAD offers six basic types of text justification and all are available with TEXT and DTEXT, and are

    normal (i.e. ranged left)
    aligned
    centred
    fitted
    middle
    right.

Refer to Fig. 26.3 which illustrates the different justifications using the DTEXT command. Justifying text is simple to achieve the sequence being

    DRAW
    DTEXT
    centred

AutoCAD prompts	Centre point
respond	**by picking the centre point for the text**.

Try each of the justifications for yourself and enter some text of your choice.

The pick points with justification are

- centred – a centre point is to be picked
- right – the right end point of the text should be picked
- aligned – two points must be selected
- middle – select the middle point
- fit – the two end points where the text is to be fitted are picked.

New alignment additions

Release 12 now has a varied range of text alignment modes which use combinations of top/middle/bottom with left/centre/right.

These are illustrated below, baseline referring to a line along which the base of the text letters lie.

The alignment can be entered (a) from the command prompt line, e.g. BL, TR, etc. or (b) by selecting Justify then BL, TR, etc.

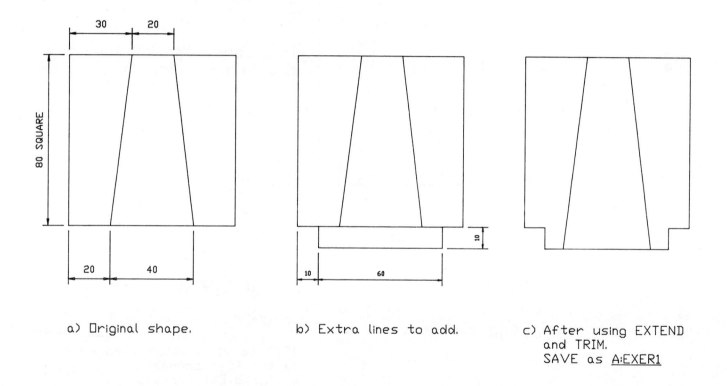

Fig. 26.1. Shape for using with TEXT.

TEXT EXERCISE   your name
                 the date

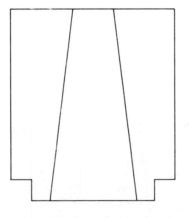

                 This component will be used
                 in a later exercise.

         AutoCAD

                           ICE CREAM is nice but cold.

AutoCAD is a draughting package.

                           TEXT can be written using either :
                           a) the TEXT command
                           b) the DTEXT command.

Fig. 26.2. TEXT exercise.

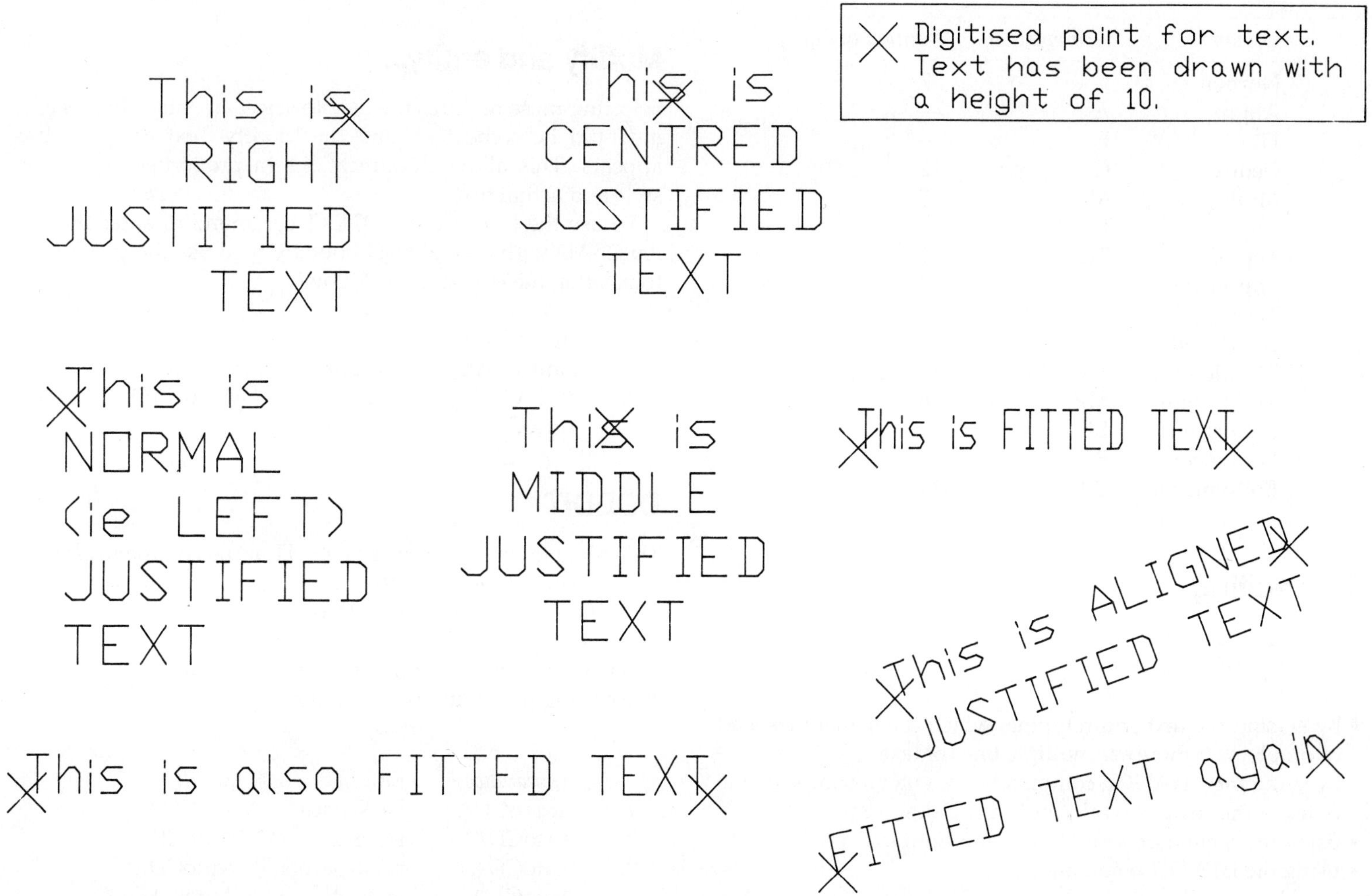

Fig. 26.3. TEXT justification.

The following table lists the abbreviations for text alignment

Option	Abbreviation	Position in example
Normal	L	7
Align	A	—
Fit	F	—
Centre	C	12
Middle	M	5
Right	R	8
Topleft	TL	1
Topcentre	TC	2
Topright	TR	3
Middleleft	ML	4
Middlecentre	MC	5
Middleright	MR	6
Bottomleft	BL	9
Bottomcentre	BC	10
Bottomright	BR	11

Text editing

Text which has been added to a drawing can be edited in a number of different ways

- by erasing the text and retyping, which can sometimes lead to problems if there are multiple lines of text
- by using the CHANGE command to re-enter a complete line of text – this always works, but can be slow
- using the menu bar with Modify and Entity...
- using the DDEDIT command.

The first two options require that the complete line of text be re-typed, while the last two options allow *single character editing*.

Modify and entity...

Selecting these requires the user to select an entity. In this case it would be some text, and the Modify Text dialogue box appears. This allows modifications in properties, e.g. layer, style and actual text.

To use the box, use the DTEXT command to enter the text AutCoAD with a height of about 15, then use the pick arrow to position the cursor (|) as follows

	Appearance	Response	Result
1.	AutCo|AD	backspace	AutCAD
2.	Aut|CAD	enter o	AutoCAD
3.	AutoCAD	pick OK	

DDEDIT

This is obtained by entering DDEDIT at the command prompt line. When entered, the user as prompted to *select a TEXT or ATTDEF object*. When the text is selected, the Edit Text dialogue box appears and editing is as described above.

As an example, enter the text AtuoCDA and then DDEDIT. The editing procedure is as follows

	Appearance	Response	Result
1.	Atu|oCDA	backspace	AtoCDA
2.	A|toCDA	enter u	AutoCDA
3.	AutoCDA|	backspace	AutoCD
4.	AutoC|D	enter A	AutoCAD
5.	AutoCAD	pick OK	

80 *Beginning AutoCAD*

❏ Summary

1. TEXT allows only one line to be entered at a time.
2. DTEXT allows multiple lines of text to be entered as well as allowing the user to view the text as it is being typed.
3. Text can be entered with varying size and at different angles.
4. Text can have different STYLES (later).
5. The 'BACKSPACE' key will correct errors as the text is being entered at the keyboard.
6. The text start point can be entered (a) from the keyboard, e.g. 30,30, (b) digitised using the puck and (c) referenced to an existing entity with OSNAP.
7. Justification (alignment) of text is possible.
8. DTEXT is probably more useful than TEXT.
9. Single character text editing is possible, and the DDEDIT option is recommended.

Activity

Attempt Tutorials 17 and 18 using your standard sheet A:STDA3, i.e. select the Files, Open... option, and enter the drawing name as **A:TUT17=A:STDA3**. Use the correct layers for outlines, centre lines and text.

27. Hatching

Hatching (or sectioning) must be drawn by the user. It is a DRAW command, and AutoCAD has several hatch 'patterns' available for the user. The hatch command with Release 12 has been updated, and the new dialogue boxes offer a great improvement over previous versions.

AutoCAD Release 12 has two hatch commands, **HATCH** and **BHATCH** and we will spend some time in this section using both of these commands.

The hatch command

Refer to Fig. 27.1, and draw a 50 unit square and then multiple copy it to the 11 other positions as shown. Draw in the smaller squares in the top row.

1. Select from the screen menu

    DRAW
    HATCH:

    AutoCAD prompts   `Pattern (? or name/U, style)`
    respond   **pick u** (for user), or enter u at prompt line.
    AutoCAD prompts   `Angle for crosshatch lines <?>`
    enter   **45<R>**
    AutoCAD prompts   `Spacing between lines <1>`
    enter   **3<R>**
    AutoCAD prompts   `Double hatch area <N>`
    enter   **N<R>** (i.e. no crosshatching).
    AutoCAD prompts   `Select objects`
    respond   **pick the 4 lines in (a) then <R>**
                      note that lines picked will change appearance.

    The hatching should then fill the square as Fig 27.1(a).

2. Now select **HATCH** then **u** and leave the 45,3,N replies as before. At the `Select objects` prompt, enter **w** and window the second square in the top row. Observe the hatch result.
3. Select **HATCH** then **u,o** and accept the 45,3,N defaults. Now window the third square (c) and note the effect.
4. Repeat the **HATCH** command with **u,i** and window (d).

The above sequence is the basic hatch procedure, the **U** meaning **USER**. Entering U allows the user to define their own hatch pattern angle and line spacing. Using **u,o** will hatch 'outer areas' only, while **u,i** will 'ignore' all entities inside the selected shape.

Using AutoCAD's existing hatch patterns

As stated previously AutoCAD has hatch patterns which are

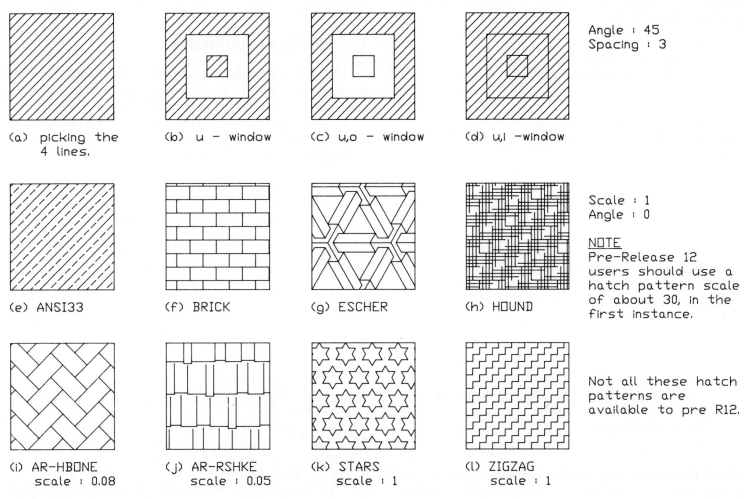

Fig. 27.1. Hatching 1.

available for the user. These patterns can be viewed (described later) or listed by selecting **HATCH** then **?**. By entering **<R>** to the prompt, a list of the available hatch patterns will be obtained, e.g.

ANGLE	angle steel
ANSI31	ANSI Iron, Brick, Stone masonry
......	
......	
AR-RSHKE	roof wood shake texture
AR-SAND	random dot pattern
......	
......	
INSUL	insulation material
LINE	parallel horizontal lines
......	
......	
TRIANG	equilateral Triangles
ZIGZAG	staircase effect

These hatch patterns can be used by selecting **HATCH:**

AutoCAD prompts	Pattern (?...)
enter	**ANSI33<R>**
AutoCAD prompts	Scale for pattern <1>
enter	**1<R>**
AutoCAD prompts	Angle for pattern <0>
enter	**0<R>**
AutoCAD prompts	Select objects
enter	**w and window (e)**

The selected square should then be hatched with the ANSI33 hatch pattern. Repeat the above hatch sequence, using pattern names of BRICK, ESCHER and HOUND, keeping the same pattern scale of 1 and an angle of 0. Use the window option when selecting the objects, and you should have hatching as Fig. 27.1(e)–(h).

The BHATCH command

BHATCH (for Boundary Hatch) is a new Release 12 command. It uses dialogue boxes which we will investigated in more detail later. The command can be selected from either (a) the on-screen menu – **BHATCH: or** (b) the menu bar – **Draw** then **Hatch...**.

The following is the sequence for using the command

1. Select **Draw** then **Hatch...**.
2. From the dialogue box, pick the **Hatch Options...**.
3. Check that Stored Hatch Patterns is active (black square).
4. Pick the **Pattern...** box.
5. The hatch pattern icons will then appear.
6. Pick next, then select the **AR-HBONE** icon.
7. The screen will return to the Hatch Options with the name **AR-HBONE** in the Pattern... box.
8. Check the **Scale** and **Angle** values by referring to Fig. 27.1(i).
9. Pick the **OK** box when your values are as required.
10. The screen returns to the Boundary Hatch dialogue.
11. Pick the **Select Objects** box.
12. At the command prompt line, enter **w** and window square (i).
13. The screen returns to the BHATCH dialogue.
14. Select the **Preview Hatch** box and check if your hatch pattern is to your requirements.
15. Press **<RETURN>**
16. Pick the **Apply** box to hatch the square, or alter the Scale and Angle values if necessary.

17. The square should be hatched with the AR-HBONE pattern.

While the above procedure may seem involved, it is actually relatively simple to use, and will become second nature after a short time. The dialogue boxes are aids to the user, and the 'preview hatch' is an invaluable aid, as it allows the user to 'see' the actual hatching before it is applied. This lets the user change values for scale and angle if necessary.

Repeat the above process for the three other patterns shown in Fig. 27.1(j)–(l) using the given names. Use the value for the scale as given.

Notes

One of the major differences in Release 12 as compared to earlier versions is in the scale pattern value. In the new version a small value is used, while earlier versions used a large value. With the earlier versions, entering too small a value for the scale pattern could actually result in the disk space becoming full. With the change to a small value, this problem has almost been eliminated, but I would still stress that when using Scale Pattern values take care. It is better to enter a larger scale pattern value and then work downwards to obtain the correct figure for your requirements, than enter a value which is too big. The preview hatch option allows the user to observe the hatch effect without actually hatching.

Using the dialogue boxes

There are two BHATCH dialogue boxes, these being the Boundary Hatch box – when command is selected and the Hatch Options box – from the Hatch Options box.

These two dialogue boxes are aids to the user, and allow users to enter user-defined patterns or stored hatch patterns.

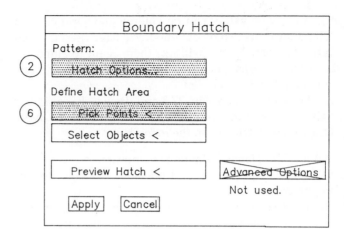

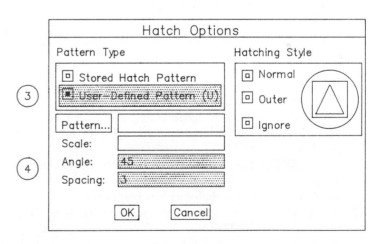

Fig. 27.2.

The scale and angle values can be entered and a preview of the hatch pattern can also be obtained. We have used the dialogue boxes previously, but will use them again to enter our own (U) hatch patterns. The dialogue boxes are shown in Fig. 27.2 but not all detail is included.

To use the boxes, refer to Fig. 27.3 and draw a shape similar to that given. Copy it to two other places on the screen. Now select **Draw** then **Hatch...** from the menu bar.

1. The Boundary Hatch dialogue box appears.
2. Select the Hatch Options, and the screen changes to this dialogue box.
3. Make the User-Defined Pattern active by picking it, and the black square indicator should move to this row.
4. Change the angle to 45, and the spacing to 3. This is achieved by placing the pick arrow at the right end of the figure and using the BACKSPACE key to delete the value in the space. The user then enters the required value.
5. Pick the OK box, and the screen returns to the first dialogue box.
6. Select the Pick Points box and the screen will return to the drawing editor.
7. By referring to Fig. 27.3, pick a point as shown in the top row figure within the innermost shape.
8. Note the change in appearance of certain entities.
9. AutoCAD will prompt by selecting everything visible..., analysing the selected data... and selecting an internal point....
10. Enter <RETURN> to signify that you are not picking any more internal points.
11. The Boundary Hatch dialogue box reappears.
12. Select the Preview box to check your hatching is as required then <RETURN>.
13. Select Apply if hatching is correct, or else repeat the process from step 2.
14. Now try and hatch the other two shapes as given in Fig. 27.3 using the above procedure. It will be necessary to pick two internal points when the Pick Points option is selected.
15. Hopefully if everything has progressed satisfactory, your final drawing will be as Fig. 27.3.

Exercise

Hatching with the dialogue boxes is easy, but it does take practice to become familiar with using them. As another example we will hatch the shape which was made during the text exercise. This should have been saved as A:EXER1, so open this file and refer to Fig. 27.4. We want to hatch the two areas as shown

1. Select **Draw** then **Hatch...** (or **BHATCH:** from screen menu).
2. Select Hatch Options... and make the User-Defined Pattern active with 45 angle and 2 spacing, then OK.
3. Select the Pick Points and pick point 1 as shown. Note line appearance changes.
4. Return to the dialogue box, select Preview and Apply if the hatching is as required.
5. Repeat the process for the 'other side'.

Before leaving this exercise, I would recommend that the you spend some time with the hatch command before proceeding to the tutorials. Draw some shapes consisting of lines, circles and arcs, and then hatch areas within these shapes. Use both the HATCH and BHATCH commands and become familiar with the dialogue boxes. Try and hatch using your own (U) hatch patterns, changing the angle and line spacing until you know what each does. Also select different patterns from the icon menus, and investigate the scale pattern effect.

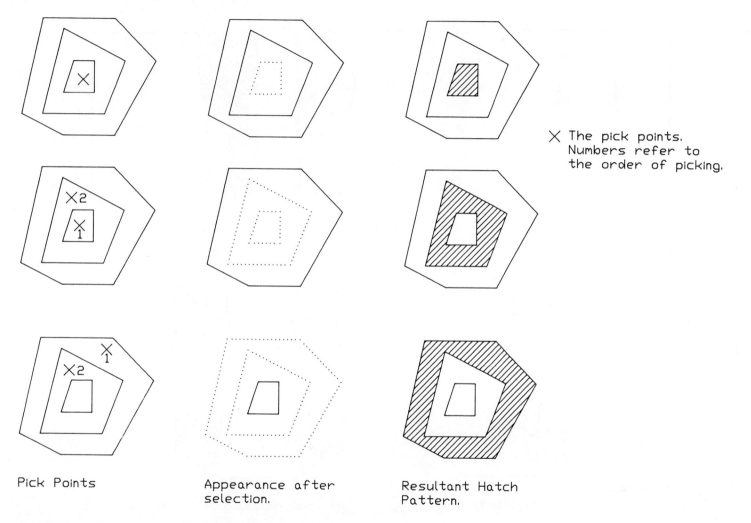

Fig. 27.3. Hatching 2 – using the BHATCH dialogue boxes.

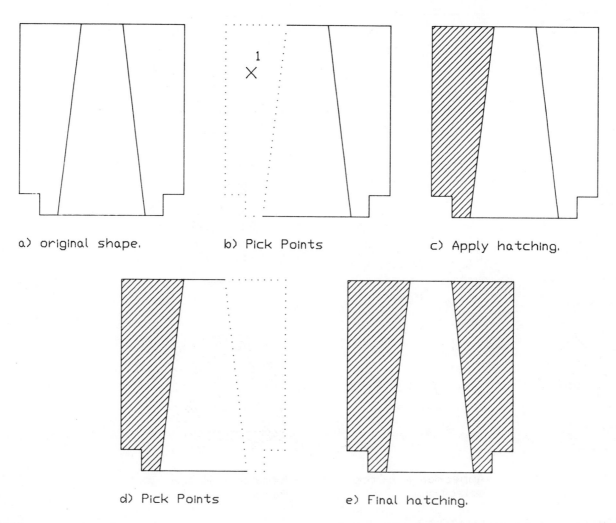

Fig. 27.4. Hatching a component.

❏ Summary

1. Hatching is obtained with the DRAW commands HATCH: or BHATCH:.
2. There are several named hatch patterns available to the user.
3. The user can enter their own hatch patterns with the U option.
4. The use of dialogue boxes greatly simplifies the hatch command.
5. All hatching should be on its own layer – in our case the layer is SECT.
6. The BHATCH: command allows three hatch methods
   (a) automatic boundary tracing
   (b) object selection
   (c) a combination of tracing and selection
7. The BHATCH: dialogue box is 'split' into two areas
   (a) the top area controls the Hatch Pattern
   (b) the bottom area controls the Boundary definition.
8. Options available with BHATCH: are
   (a) Hatch Options – allows the user to select the required hatch pattern and style
   (b) Pick Points – prompts the user for an internal point and then traces around the area to be hatched
   (c) Select Objects – prompts for the selection of objects and adds them to the selection set
   (d) Advanced Options – not considered in the book.
9. LTSCALE does not affect the hatch pattern.

Activity

Spend some time on Tutorials 19–24 which all involve hatching. Use layers in all these drawings and draw the hatching on the SECT layer.

28. The BREAK command

It is often required to 'split' entities into a number of distinct parts, and one method of achieving this is to use BREAK. We will demonstrate this command using the **A:EXER1** drawing used and saved with the text exercise, so **Open...**, etc. and refer to Fig 28.1 on the next page.

Before proceeding, check that the top and bottom horizontal lines have been drawn as single entities. If they have not, then erase the entities making up these lines, and draw in two single lines.

Select from the menu

EDIT
BREAK

AutoCAD prompts	Select objects
respond	**pick line d**1 and note the complete line changes.
AutoCAD prompts	Enter second point (or F for first point)
respond	**pick First** from the menu (or enter F at prompt).
AutoCAD prompts	Enter first point ****
respond	**INTersect** **pick d2**
AutoCAD prompts	Enter second point
respond	**pick @** from the menu.

Nothing appears to have happened, but the top horizontal line has been 'split' into two parts. This is evident if you select ERASE and pick the smaller left hand portion of the line. It will be erased. Try it and then enter **u<R>** immediately to restore it.

The @ symbol is very useful with the BREAK command, as it is used to indicate that *the second point to be selected is the same as the first point*, thus eliminating the need to select ****INT, etc.

Repeat the BREAK command digitising line d3, then OSNAP INT d4. The bottom horizontal line will be split into two parts.

It may be required to use the BREAK command twice at the same point. Draw the other shape in Fig. 28.1, the triangle being from point 1–2–3, and the rectangle from point 4–5–6–7. We want to use the BREAK command at the points where the triangle and rectangle meet, and then MOVE the inner shape as shown. To achieve this, BREAK must be used eight times, twice at each intersected point. Can you reason out why this is?

❏ Summary

1. BREAK is an EDIT command used to 'split' entities into parts.
2. It is possible to obtain the same effect as BREAK by using the TRIM command and then drawing back in the trimmed entities. This is sometimes as quick as using BREAK.

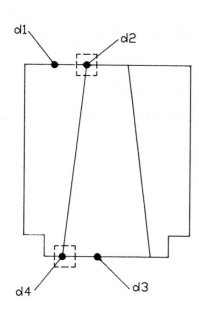
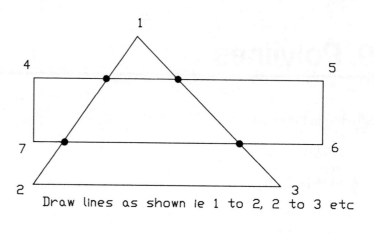
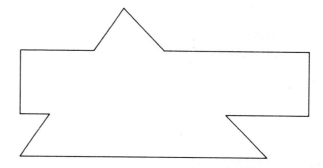

Fig. 28.1. BREAK command.

The BREAK command

29. Polylines

1. Select from the menu

   DRAW
   next
   PLINE:

   enter   50,170   for the start point
   then   @50,0
            @0,50
            @-50,0
            @0,-50   to complete square
            <RETURN>   to end sequence.

   Now select from the menu

   EDIT
   next
   FILLET
   radius and enter **10 <R>**
   polyline
   pick any line drawn

   The result should be as Fig. 29.1(a) with three corners of the square having the fillet radius added.

2. Draw a second square with

   PLINE:
   140,170   the start point

   @50,0
   @0,50
   @-50,0
   close   from the screen.

   Repeat the **EDIT–next–FILLET–radius–10–polyline–pick point** sequence and the result should be as Fig. 29.1(b), i.e. all four corners should have been filleted.

   This difference is due to the close option in Fig. 29.1(b) having been selected, instead of **<RETURN>** in Fig. 29.1(a).

3. Now draw a polyshape from

   40,40
   @200,0
   @0,100
   @-200,0
   close

   This time select

   EDIT
   CHAMFER
   distance and enter **30 <R>** for both distances
   polyline
   pick a point on any line drawn
   EDIT
   next
   FILLET

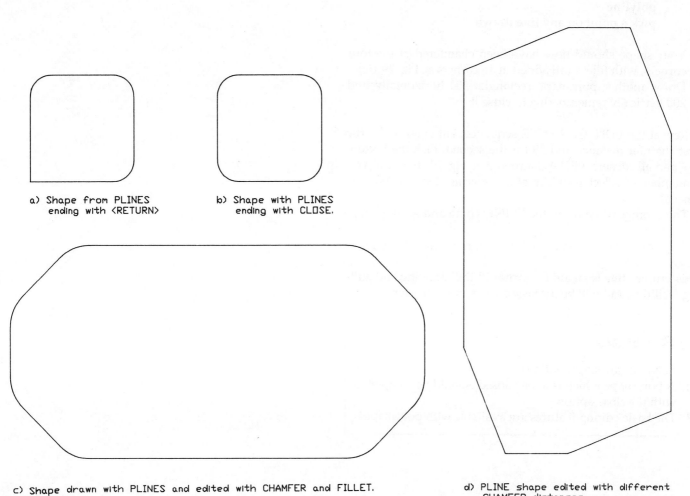

Fig. 29.1. Polylines.

radius and enter **20 <R>**
polyline
pick a point on any line drawn

Your shape should now have been chamfered at the four corners, with fillet radii added at 16 corners as Fig. 29.1(c).

4. Draw another polyshape rectangle, 100 horizontally and 200 vertically remembering to **close** it.

Repeat the EDIT–CHAMFER sequence, but enter 50 for the first chamfer distance and 20 for the second. Pick the bottom line and all corners will be chamfered as Fig. 29.1(d) – did you remember to select **polyline** after entering the chamfer distances?

The prompt when using the PLINE: command is quite long

```
Arc/Close/Halfwidth/Length/Undo/Width
```

This prompt line is an aid to further PLINE drawing and editing facilities, and will be discussed in the next chapter.

❏ Summary

1. Polylines are single entities.
2. A polyshape which is to be 'closed' should be completed with the close option.
3. The basic editing features are available with polyshapes.

30. Adding arc segments during PLINE definition

Erase all existing entities from the screen (saving if you want) and then refer to Fig. 30.1. We shall now draw this shape using polylines.
Select from the menu

DRAW
next
PLINE:

AutoCAD prompts	From point
enter	**40,40<R>** (point 1)
AutoCAD prompts	Arc/Close/Halfwidth/Length...<Endpoint>
select	**Width**
AutoCAD prompts	Starting width<0.00>
enter	**10<R>**
AutoCAD prompts	Ending width<10.00>
enter	**5<R>**
AutoCAD prompts	Arc/Close...
enter	**@200,0<R>** (point 2)
AutoCAD prompts	Arc/...
select	**Arc** and note menu change
AutoCAD prompts	Angle/CEntre/Close...
enter	**@50,50<R>** (point 3)
AutoCAD prompts	Angle...
select	**contline** and note menu change
AutoCAD prompts	Arc/Close...
select	**Width**
AutoCAD prompts	Starting width<5.00>
enter	**5<R>**
AutoCAD prompts	Ending width<5.00>
enter	**0<R>**
AutoCAD prompts	Arc/Close...
enter	**@0,100<R>** (point 4)
AutoCAD prompts	Arc...
enter	**210,240<R>** (point 5)
AutoCAD prompts	Arc...
select	**Width**
AutoCAD prompts	Starting width<0.00>
enter	**0<R>**
AutoCAD prompts	Ending width<0.00>
enter	**5<R>**
AutoCAD prompts	Arc...
enter	**210,150<R>** (point 6)
AutoCAD prompts	Arc...
select	**Arc** and note menu change
AutoCAD prompts	Angle/CEntre...
enter	**160,150<R>** (point 7)
AutoCAD prompts	Angle...
select	**CEntre**
AutoCAD prompts	centre point
enter	**@-50,0<R>** (point 8)
AutoCAD prompts	Angle...
select	**angle**
AutoCAD prompts	Included angle

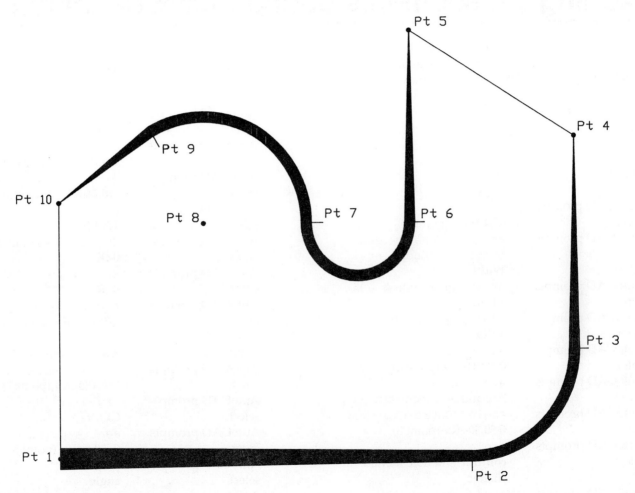

Fig. 30.1. Polyline commands.

96 *Beginning AutoCAD*

enter	**120<R>** (point 9)
AutoCAD prompts	`Angle...`
select	**contline**
AutoCAD prompts	`Arc/Close...`
select	**Width**
AutoCAD prompts	`Starting width<5.00>`
enter	**5<R>**
AutoCAD prompts	`Ending width<5.00>`
enter	**0<R>**
AutoCAD prompts	`Arc...`
enter	**40,160 <R>** (point 10)
AutoCAD prompts	`Arc...`
select	**Close** (point 1 again).

That's all there is to it!

With a bit of luck, your polyshape will be the same as Fig. 30.1. I admit that there seems to be a lot in this sequence, but I have laboured the prompts as they are important when adding arc segments.

The problem with a complicated polyshape is that if you have made a mistake and erase it, you will have to begin from the start point and go through the whole process again. It is only through usage that you become familiar with all the various options available with PLINE.

Save this drawing, as it will be used to demonstrate the editing of polylines.

31. PEDIT

Polylines can be erased with the normal ERASE command, but they have their own editing command, which gives extra facilities not available to ordinary entities. This command is PEDIT.

Open your drawing of the polyline shape made in the last chapter and then select

    EDIT
    ERASE
    pick any point
    <RETURN>

The complete shape will be erased. This is because it is a polyline – all the line and arc segments are considered as one complete entity.

Now select **OOPS** to restore the shape.

We will now use the PEDIT command to change certain aspects of this original drawing, so refer to Fig. 31.1.

Constant width

Select from the menu

    EDIT
    next
    PEDIT

AutoCAD prompts	`Select objects`
select	**any point on shape and <RETURN>**
AutoCAD prompts	`Open/Join/Width...`
select	**Width**
AutoCAD prompts	`Enter new width for all segments`
enter	**3<R>**

The shape should now have been redrawn with this constant width as Fig. 31.1(b).

Straightening a polyshape

You should still be in the PEDIT menu, so

    select   **Decurve**

and the polyshape will be drawn without any curves [as shown in Fig. 31.1(c)].

Fitting a curve to a polyshape

Again you should still be in the PEDIT menu, so

    select   **Fit Curv**

The result of this option may seem rather strange, and is at

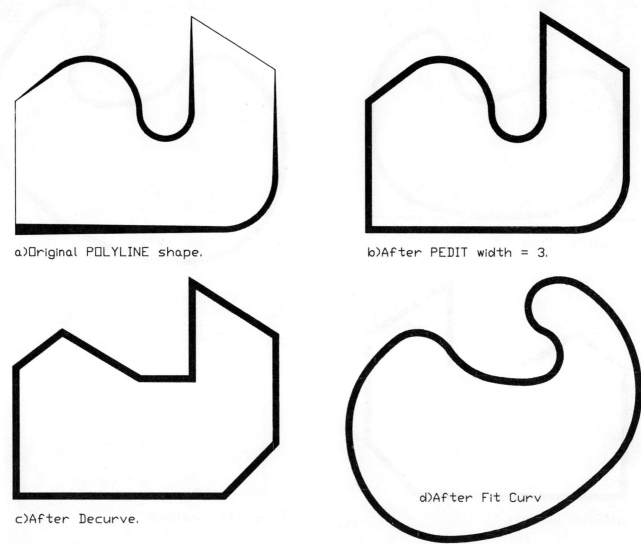

Fig.31.1. PEDIT 1.

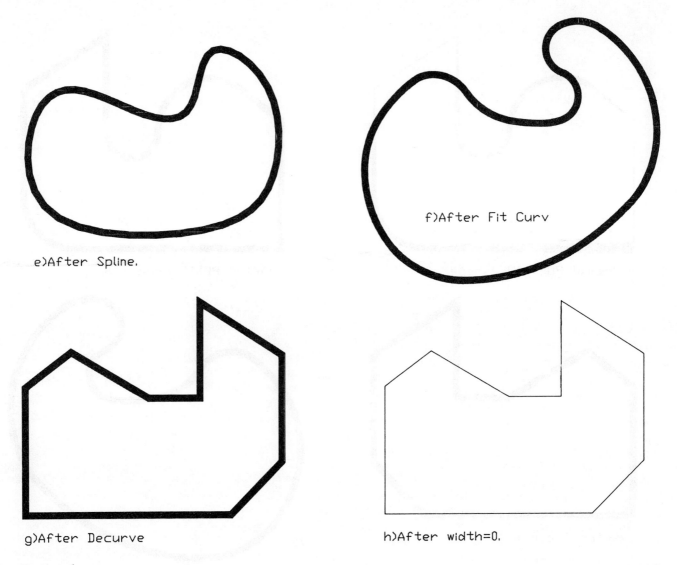

Fig. 31.1. *Continued.*

present beyond the scope of this book. It is doubtful if the user would want to use these commands, but I have included them for observation purposes.

Completion

To complete this exercise

    select   **Spline**   Fig. 31.1(e)
                  Fit Curv   (f)
                  Decurve   (g)
                  Width and enter 0<R>   (h)

Other PEDIT commands

Refer to Fig. 31.2 and draw four shapes using PLINE similar to those in the top row. Select PEDIT and follow the sequence below

(a) **PEDIT**
    pick a point in Fig. 31.2(a) then **<R>**
    Close
(b) **PEDIT**
    pick a point in Fig. 31.2(b) then **<R>**
    Open
(c) **PEDIT**
    pick a point in Fig. 31.2(c) then **<R>**
    EdVrtx
    use N to move to any vertex
    use M and position the vertex at another point
(d) **PEDIT**
    pick a point in Fig. 31.2(d) then **<R>**
    Spline

Most of the PEDIT commands will not be used by the reader at this level, and are included to show the versatility of polylines.

❏ *Summary*

1. A polyline is a single entity.
2. Complicated shapes can be made from PLINE line and arc segments.
3. Polylines can be OFFSET, FILLETED and CHAMFERED.
4. Polylines have their own editing facilities – PEDIT.
5. PEDIT is a very powerful editing facility.

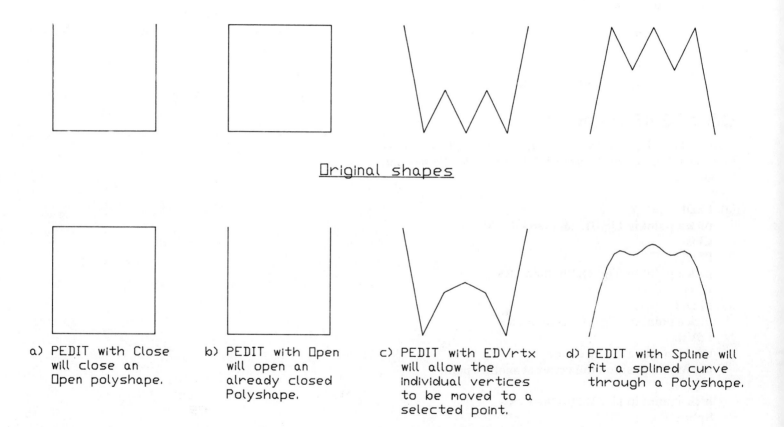

Fig. 31.2. PEDIT 2.

32. User exercise 3

Use polylines to construct the drawing shown in Fig. 32.1, with OFFSET, FILLET and CHAMFER.

Activity

Tutorials 25–27 can now be attempted. They have all been drawn using the PLINE command.

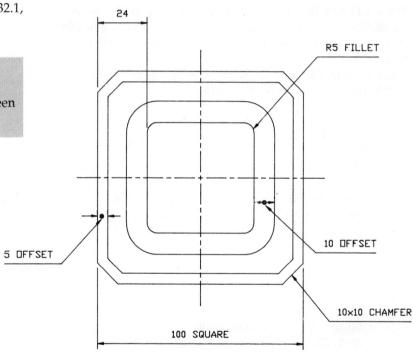

Fig. 32.1.

33. Polygons

AutoCAD has the facility to draw polygons with one command. They are polylines, and can be drawn with any number of sides and can be inscribed or circumscribed in circles, i.e. A/C or A/F.

Refer to Fig. 33.1, and we shall draw six different polygons. POLYGON is a DRAW command, so select

DRAW
next
POLYGON

1. Prompt: number of sides   enter: **6<R>**
   prompt: edge or centre   select: **edge**
   prompt: first point   enter: **70,160<R>**
   prompt: second point   enter: **@30,0<R>**

2. Repeat (1) with **8** sides, with

   edge
   90,40   as first point
   @30<25   for second point

3. Prompt: number of sides   enter: **5<R>**
   prompt: edge or centre   enter: **190,190<R>** as centre
   prompt: I or C   select: **I-scribed**
   prompt: radius   enter: **30<R>**

4. Repeat (3) with **7** sides, with

   190,80 as centre
   I-scribed
   @20<15 as radius

5. Prompt: number of sides   enter: **8<R>**
   prompt: edge or centre   enter: **290,190<R>** as centre
   prompt: I or C   select: **C-scribed**
   prompt: radius   enter: **40<R>**

6. Repeat (5) with **4** sides, with

   290,80 as centre
   C-scribed
   @27.5<-45 as radius

Your drawing should now resemble Fig. 33.1.

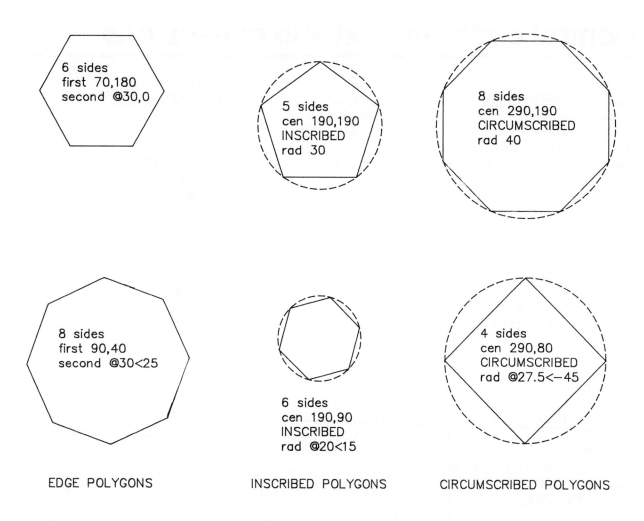

Fig. 33.1. Drawing polygons.

34. Control codes for text and dimensions

The drawings completed so far have had various items of text underlined, as well as circular shapes having had the diameter symbol attached. These effects are obtained by using AutoCAD's control codes. Control codes allow the user to underline and overscore text and dimensions, as well as adding certain symbols.

The following control codes can be used:

%%O	toggles the OVERSCORE on/off.
%%U	toggles the UNDERSCORE on/off.
%%D	draws the DEGREES (angle or temperature) symbol.
%%P	draws a PLUS/MINUS symbol.
%%C	draws the DIAMETER symbol.
%%%	draws the PERCENTAGE symbol.

Open a new file, and refer to Fig. 34.1.

1. Select DRAW
   DTEXT
   enter 50,210<R>   for text start point
   enter 15<R>   for text height
   enter 0<R>   for text rotation
   enter %%UAutoCAD%%U<R>   as text
   enter <RETURN>   next line of text
   enter <RETURN>   to complete command.

2. Select DTEXT
   280,210
   10
   0
   96.5%%DF
   <R>
   <R>

3. Select DTEXT
   220,160
   10
   0
   %%C50
   <R>
   <R>

Now try and complete the rest of the text in Fig. 34.1.

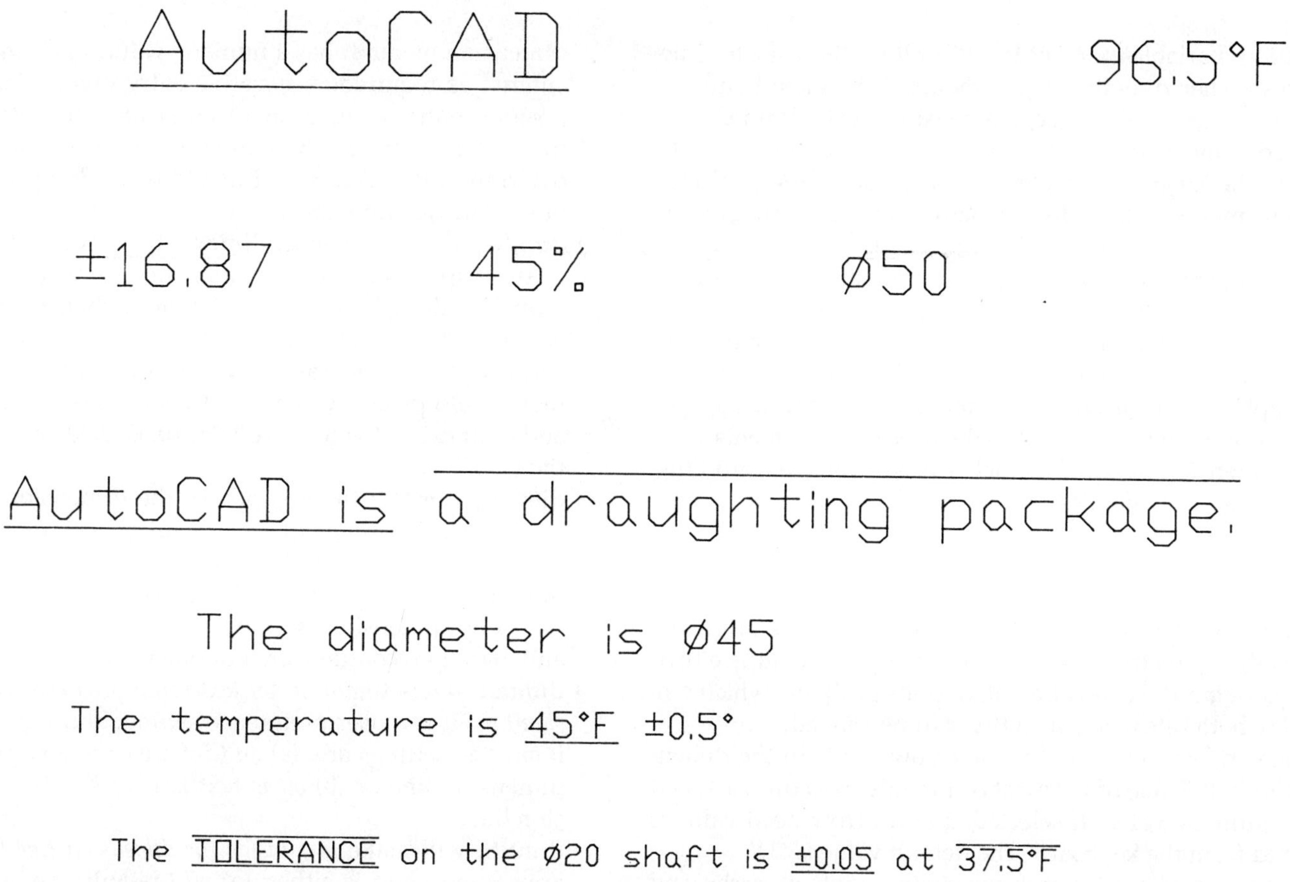

AutoCAD   96.5°F

±16.87   45%   Ø50

AutoCAD is a draughting package.

The diameter is Ø45

The temperature is 45°F ±0.5°

The TOLERANCE on the Ø20 shaft is ±0.05 at 37.5°F

Fig. 34.1. Using CONTROL codes.

35. DIMVARS

Dimension Variables (or DIMVARS) allow the user to 'fine-tune' his or her drawing requirements. They include dimension text size, arrow size, dimension text position and dimension line features. As the name implies they will be found in the **DIM:** screen menu, and if **Dim Vars** is selected from the menu, a long list of names will appear: dimcen, dimtxt, etc. Most of these will not be needed by the user, and most companies will have set their standard sheet to their own personal requirements as regards dimensions. However, several of the variables are very useful, and will assist the user to produce a 'more professional' CAD drawing. The object of this chapter is to introduce the more commonly used variables, and how they can be set to the user's requirements.

The dimension variables which we will consider are illustrated in Figs 35.1 and 35.2.

- **dimalt:** displays *alternative units* as well as those originally selected, e.g. metric and imperial together. Dimalt is either: (a) *off* (default), i.e. no alternative units or (b) *on* which will display both sets when an entity is dimensioned.
- **dimasz:** refers to the size of the arrow-heads in the dimension lines. It is one of the most commonly used dimvars, and has a numeric value. If selected, a new arrow head value is entered from the keyboard. The default value is '3?'
- **dimcen:** gives lines through the centre points of circles and arcs when *centre mark, radius, diameter* are selected from the dimension menu. It has a numeric value, and a new value is entered as required. A negative entry gives a large cross, a positive entry gives a small cross and no entry gives no mark at the centre. The magnitude of the number entered determines the cross size. I like to use a dimcen value of +2 or +3. The default value is –3.
- **dimdle, dimdli, dimexe, dimexo:** these four variables refer to the appearance of the actual dimension line offsets, for example, the incremental difference when using baseline, etc. The AutoCAD reference manual illustrates their use, and it is only with scale drawings and odd paper sizes that they would probably be used. They require a numeric input, and their default values are 1.25, 10.00, 2.50 and 2.50, respectively.
- **dimse1, dimse2:** these suppress the dimension line extension and are either: (a) *off* (default), i.e. extension line is drawn or (b) *on* which means that no extension line is drawn. These are useful variables to alter, especially if more than one dimension is being taken from a common point and baseline/continue are not practical.
- **dimtad:** refers to *dimension text being placed above the dimension line*. It is a user preference setting, and I generally have it *on*. The settings are: (a) *on* (default), i.e. text placed above dimension line or (b) *off* is text is placed inside the dimension line.
- **dimtih:** will make *text inside the dimension line horizontal* in appearance, and is either: (a) *off* (default), i.e. inside text is not horizontal or (b) *on* will make the text inside horizontal.

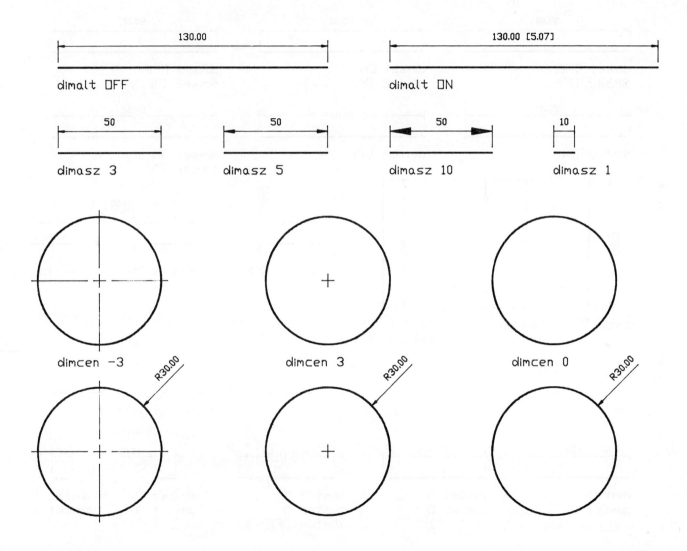

Fig. 35.1. DIMVARS 1.

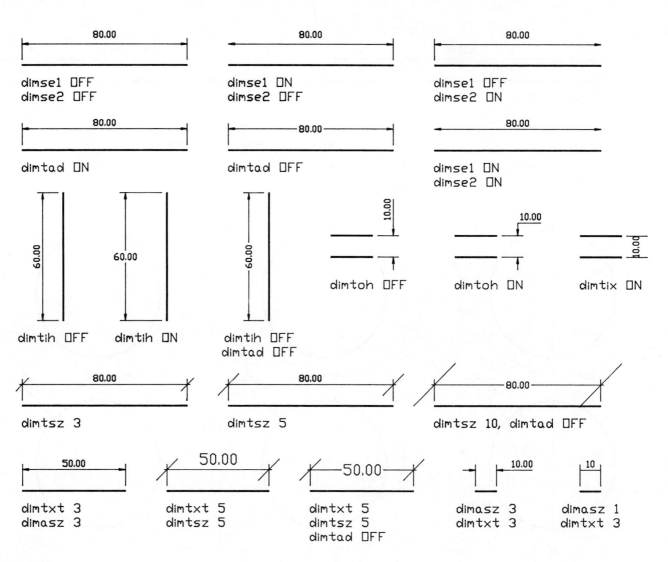

Fig. 35.2. DIMVARS 2.

- **dimtoh:** makes *text outside the dimension line horizontal*, and is: (a) *off* (default), i.e. text outside is not horizontal or (b) *on* which will make outside text horizontal.
- **dimtsx:** allows **ticks** to be used instead of arrow heads at the ends of the dimension lines. It is either: (a) 0 (default), i.e. no ticks or (b) a value in which case ticks will be drawn, and arrow-heads will not. The magnitude of the value entered determines the size of the ticks.
- **dimtxt:** this refers to the *size of the actual dimension text*. It requires a numeric value and is usually set to 3.

When using dimension variables, more than one can be set at the one time, e.g. dimse1 could be set to *on*, dimtih set to *on*, dimtxt set to 10. The problem with altering these variables is remembering what the original default value was, and also what actual variables were altered.

It is only with a great deal of patience and practice that the user will become familiar with all of the variables (I would suggest that the majority of them will never be used). It is thus recommended that you sit at your system one day with the AutoCAD manual, draw some entities, and work through the list of DIMVARS to see what the effects of altering the values has on your drawing.

36. Tolerances and limits

In engineering drawings many dimensions must include tolerances and limits. These can be included in the actual dimension by using the following dimension variables

dimlim: sets limits on or off (default)
dimtol: sets tolerances on or off (default)
dimtp: sets the *plus tolerance/limit*, e.g. +0.05
dimtm: sets the *minus tolerance/limit*, e.g. −0.02

Dimtp and dimtm require a numeric entry from the keyboard, *but the + or − symbol is not entered,* i.e. dimtm of 0.03 will be taken as a tolerance/limit of −0.03. Dimtol and dimlim both have a default of off, no limits or tolerances being shown when dimensioning. Both of these variables can be off at the same time, but not on at the same time, i.e. *if dimtol is on, then dimlim is off* and vice-versa. Turning one on will automatically toggle the other off.

Refer to Fig. 36.1 and draw ten lines of length 100, and we will add the dimensions shown.

Lines (a) with dimtp=0.05 and dimtm=0.02

Select from the screen menu

DIM:
Dim Vars
next
next

dimtm and enter **0.02<R>**
dimtp and enter **0.05<R>**
dimtol and select ON
Dim Menu
horizontl
dimension top left line
accept default <100.0000>
previous
Dim Vars
next
dimlim and select **ON**
Dim Menu
horizontl
dimension top right line
accept default <100.0000>

Repeat the above procedure for the other pairs of lines, using the dimtp and dimtm values given. Note that Fig. 36.1(a)–(d) have units set to four decimal places and Fig. 36.1(e) has the units set to two decimal places.

Note

1. New values must be entered every time dimtp and dimtm change.
2. Tolerances and limits will only work with the default dimension value, i.e. you will not get tolerances/limits if you enter your own dimension value from the keyboard. Try it for yourself.

Activity

Attempt Tutorial 28.

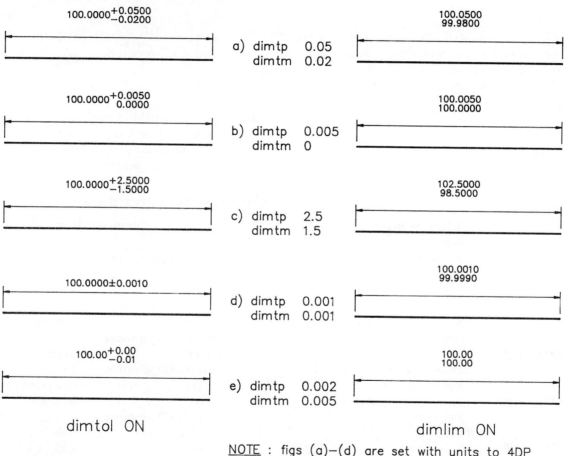

Fig. 36.1. Tolerances and limits.

37. Arrays

ARRAY is an EDIT command and allows the user to make multiple copies of single entities, polylines or shapes. These can be in either rectangular or polar (circular) patterns.

Refer to Fig. 37.1 and make the basic shape shown, then copy it to the three places indicated by S1, S2 and S3.

Rectangular array

Select from the menu
    EDIT
    ARRAY

AutoCAD prompts	Select objects
respond	**Select Objects**
	Window
	window shape at S1
	<RETURN>
AutoCAD prompts	Rectangular or Polar array (R/P)
enter	**R<R> or pick Rectangle from screen.**
AutoCAD prompts	Number of rows (- - -)<1>
enter	**2<R>**
AutoCAD prompts	Number of columns (| | | |)<1>
enter	**4<R>**
AutoCAD prompts	Unit cell or distance between rows (- - -)
enter	**–30<R>**
AutoCAD prompts	Distance between columns (| | | |)
enter	**20<R>**

The shape at S1 will be copied seven times into a two rows by four column grid (matrix) pattern. The above is the basic prompts for all rectangular arrays. A rectangular array must have at least one row and one column, hence the <1> default.

Polar array with rotation

Repeat the ARRAY command, digitise the shape at S2, then

AutoCAD prompts	Rect or Polar array (R/P)
enter	**P<R> or pick P**
AutoCAD prompts	Centre point of array
enter	**130,100<R>**
AutoCAD prompts	Number of items
enter	**8<R>**
AutoCAD prompts	Angle to fill (+CCW, –CW)<360>
enter	**360<R>**
AutoCAD prompts	Rotate objects as they are copied<Y>
enter	**<RETURN>**, i.e. accept Y default

114   *Beginning AutoCAD*

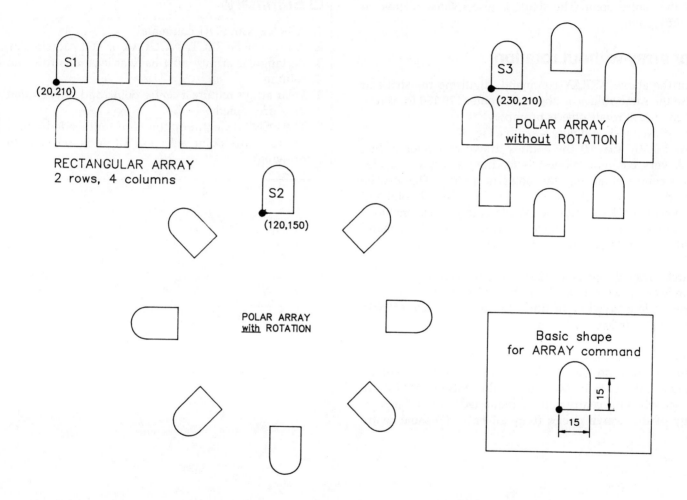

Fig. 37.1. Array 1.

A circular array will result, with the shape at S2 being copied about the centre point. The shape is also rotated relative to this centre point.

Polar array without rotation

Repeat the above ARRAY command, digitising the shape at S3. Use the same values as above, but enter **270,180** for centre point enter **N** at rotate objects prompt.

Your drawing should now resemble Fig. 37.1.

Now ERASE (Save?) the entities drawn and refer to Fig. 37.2. A very common request is to draw a series of circles about a centre point, e.g. the holes in a shaft. This can be achieved by: (a) drawing each circle at the required point and (b) using the COPY command. While both of these methods are acceptable, they are inefficient and the ARRAY command should be used. The diagrams shown are

(a) circle arrayed four times about the circle centre
(b) circle arrayed six times about the centre point
(c) the circle arrayed eight times through an angle of 240°, about the circle centre point.

Try these three drawings for yourself. The circle radii are 20 and 60, and the centre line circle radius is 40. The radius of the circle to be arrayed is 10. Make use of the **OSNAP **** Centre** sequence when the centre point is requested, and pick a point on any of the drawn circles (they all have the same centre point).

❑ Summary

1. ARRAY is an EDIT command.
2. Arrays can be RECTANGULAR or POLAR (circular).
3. Rectangular arrays must have at least one row and one column.
4. Polar arrays require a centre point, and can be rotated as they are copied.
5. The OSNAP Centre option is recommended with polar array centre point selection (if it is relevant to the drawing).

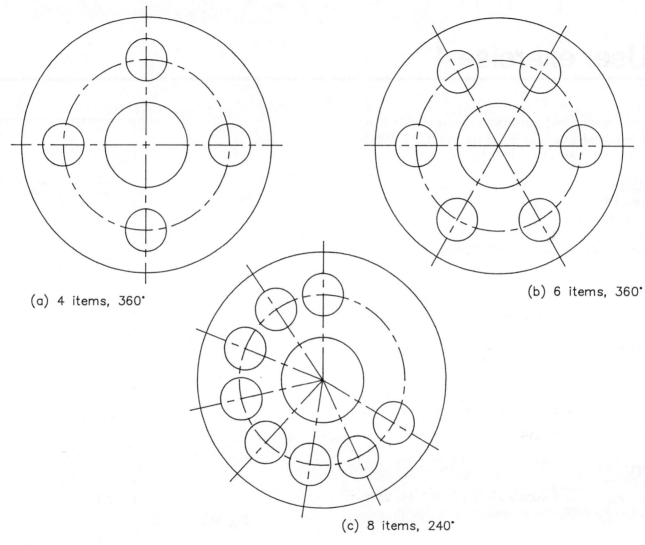

Fig. 37.2. Polar array.

Arrays

38. User exercise 4

Begin a new drawing and construct a square of side 30 units, the lower left-hand corner being at the point (110,50). Now ARRAY this square using the following sequence

    EDIT
    ARRAY
    Select Objects
    Window
    window the square then **<RETURN>**

enter

R<R>	rectangular
5<R>	rows
2<R>	columns
35<R>	row distance
35<R>	column distance.

Your drawing should be as shown in Fig. 38.1. **Save As...** for future use.

Activity

Spend some time on Tutorials 29–35 which have all been drawn using the ARRAY command.

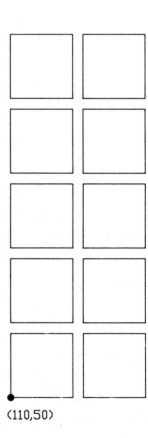

Fig. 38.1.

118   *Beginning AutoCAD*

39. The CHANGE command

The CHANGE command was used in an earlier chapter to change the linetype of a continuous line to a centre line. This method of altering linetype appearance was superseded with the introduction of layers, but the CHANGE command still has uses. We will use it to demonstrate how text can be altered, in conjunction with the ARRAY command.

Refer to Fig. 39.1 and (a) draw the given arc segment and add the single vertical line and with the text 0 (zero) centred as indicated and (b) array the line and number 0 (i) ACW, four times through 30° and (ii) CW, seven times through 60°.

We will now alter the 0 text to numbers 10, 20, ..., 100 with the CHANGE command, so

EDIT
CHANGE

AutoCAD prompts	Select objects
respond	**pick the most left 0** **<RETURN>**
AutoCAD prompts	Properties/<Change point>
respond	**<RETURN>**
AutoCAD prompts	Enter text insertion point
respond	**<RETURN>**, i.e. leave text position unchanged
AutoCAD prompts	New style or RETURN for no change
respond	**<RETURN>**
AutoCAD prompts	New height <?>
enter	**8 <R>**
AutoCAD prompts	New rotation angle <30?>
respond	**<RETURN>**
AutoCAD prompts	New text <0>
enter	**10<R>**

The number 10 should now have replaced the number 0 at the left of the arc segment.

Repeat the above sequence entering the numbers 20–100 with the following heights

10,20 at 8
30,40 at 7
50,60 at 6
70,80 at 5
90,100 at 4

Activity

Try Tutorial 35 which is quite interesting.

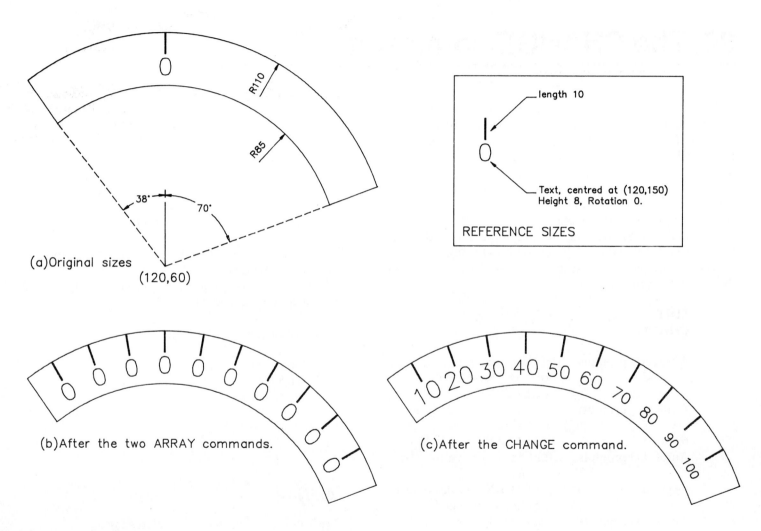

Fig. 39.1. Array with CHANGE.

40. Text fonts and styles

Text should now be added to every drawing. It may only be your name and date, but may also include titles, notes, etc. Up until now, the text has always had the same appearance but we will now investigate the possibility of altering the style of the text.

There are two new AutoCAD concepts when dealing with text, these being *fonts* and *styles*.

Font

A text font defines the pattern which is used to draw text characters. Text can be drawn in a number of different font styles, and AutoCAD is supplied with various fonts. These can be viewed in ICON from the menu bar. There are however four *basic* font styles, these being

- txt – the standard font (default)
- simplex – smoother in appearance
- complex – a multi-stroke font
- italic – italicised font.

Figure 40.1 shows the general appearance of these basic fonts as well as some text from the ICON fonts.

Style

A text style defines the parameters used to draw actual text. These parameters include the width factor, the obliquing angle, whether text is to be upside-down and so on. Text styles are defined by the user and can be called up by referencing the style name.

Note

Any text font can be used in several styles, and it is the style that is referenced by the text definition.

To 'see' what styles are available at the start of a drawing session, select

        DRAW
        DTEXT
        STYLE:
enter   **?<R>**

AutoCAD prompts   `Text style(s) to list<*>`
enter   **<RETURN>**

AutoCAD 'flips' to the text screen with the following

```
Text Styles:
Style name: STANDARD    Font file: TXT
Height:0.00    Width factor: 1.00
Obliquing angle: 0.00
Generation: Normal
Current text style: STANDARD
```

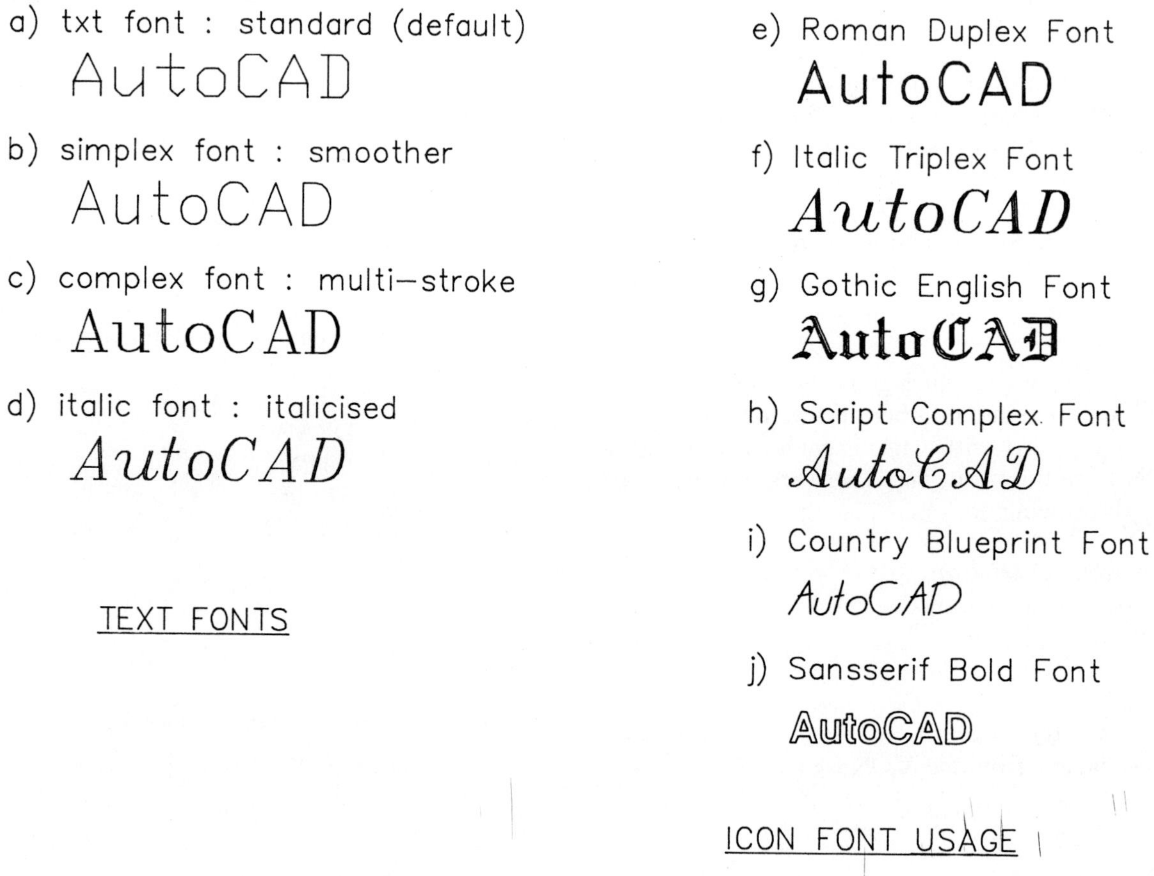

a) txt font : standard (default)
AutoCAD

b) simplex font : smoother
AutoCAD

c) complex font : multi-stroke
AutoCAD

d) italic font : italicised
AutoCAD

TEXT FONTS

e) Roman Duplex Font
AutoCAD

f) Italic Triplex Font
AutoCAD

g) Gothic English Font
AutoCAD

h) Script Complex Font
AutoCAD

i) Country Blueprint Font
AutoCAD

j) Sansserif Bold Font
AutoCAD

ICON FONT USAGE

Fig. 40.1. Text fonts.

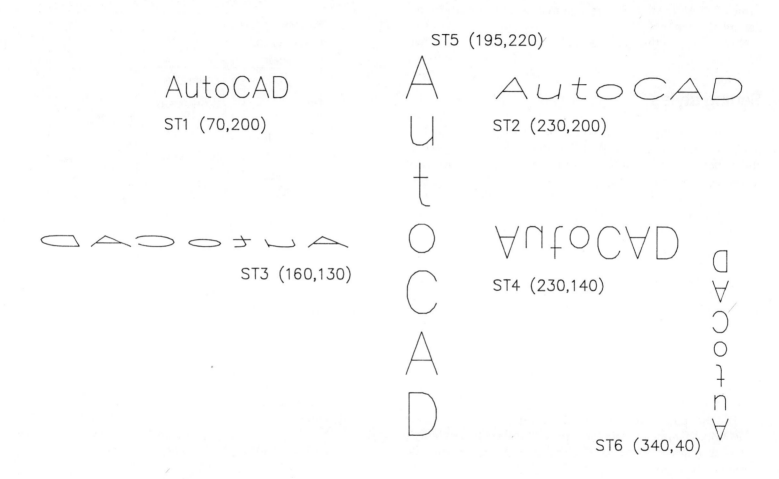

Fig. 40.2. Different text styles for one font (ROMANS). (The figures in parentheses are the start points.)

Text fonts and styles

This is the AutoCAD default style (on my machine). Note the name of STANDARD/TXT as you may want to return to this default at some time.

Now return to the drawing editor with **CTRL C** and then **F1**.

Setting styles

To show the setting of text styles, refer to Fig. 40.2 which is one text font (ROMAN SIMPLEX or ROMANS) with different styles. Before a font can be used in a drawing, it is necessary to define its STYLE, i.e. the width, whether backwards or not, and so on. This will be shown by 'making' six different styles for the one (ROMANS) font.

Select the following sequence

> **DRAW**
> **DTEXT**
> **STYLE:**

AutoCAD prompts	Text style name (or ?)
enter	**ST1\<R\>**
AutoCAD prompts	New style and the Select Font File dialogue box will be displayed (Fig. 40.3).

1. Use the pick arrow to scroll upwards until the name **ROMANS** appears, and then 'pick it'. It should turn blue.
2. Check that the name ROMANS has appeared in the **File name** box.
3. Pick the **OK** box.
4. This will set the ROMANS text font as current.
5. When this has been completed, the drawing screen re-appears and

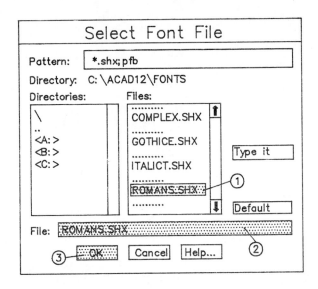

Fig. 40.3. Select Font File dialogue box.

AutoCAD prompts enter	Height<0.00> **10\<R\>**
AutoCAD prompts enter	Width factor<1.0> **0\<R\>**
AutoCAD prompts enter	Obliquing angle<0.0> **0\<R\>**
AutoCAD prompts enter	Backwards<N> **\<RETURN\>**, i.e. accept default
AutoCAD prompts	Upsidedown<N> accept default N
AutoCAD prompts	Vertical<N> accept default N
AutoCAD prompts	ST1 is now the current text style

124 *Beginning AutoCAD*

Table 40.1

Style name	ST2	ST3	ST4	ST5	ST6
Font name	ROMANS	ROMANS	ROMANS	ROMANS	ROMANS
Height	10	5	15	20	10
Width factor	2	5	1	1	1
Obliquing angle	10	30	0	0	0
Backwards	N	Y	N	N	Y
Upsidedown	N	N	Y	N	Y
Vertical	N	N	N	Y	Y

At present we will not use this newly created style, but will repeat the above sequence for the five other text styles required. Table 40.1 gives the data for these styles, so use it to answer the prompts as they appear.

If the procedure has been followed correctly, AutoCAD will now have made six new text styles. Check by selecting

        STYLE:
enter   **?<R>**
        <RETURN>

A list of the text styles available will be displayed, and the six you have just made will be shown, with the various settings stated. Return to the drawing screen and we will proceed to use these new styles.

Using styles

Any text style which has been created must be 'set' as current before it can used to draw text, so select

    DRAW
    DTEXT
    Style (N.B. not **STYLE**)

AutoCAD prompts	Style name
enter	**ST1<R>**
AutoCAD prompts	Start point
enter	**70,200<R>**
AutoCAD prompts	Rotation angle<0.00>
enter	**<RETURN>**, i.e. accept 0 default
AutoCAD prompts	Text
enter	**AutoCAD<R>**

The word 'AutoCAD' will be displayed at the start point (70,200) with the style setting for ST1, i.e. 10 high, etc. Now repeat the above sequence for the other five text styles, using the start points given in Fig. 40.1.

Using the icon fonts

AutoCAD Release 12 comes equipped with about 40 text fonts already prepared for the user to select. These cover most of the recognised text styles and some new ones. Gothic and italicised text fonts are included as are fonts for mathematics, weather symbols, map symbols, etc.

The icons can be obtained from the menu bar with

Draw
Text >
Set Style...

The Select Text Font dialogue box is then displayed as shown in Fig. 40.4. The dialogue box offers the user a chance to 'see' the appearance of the different text fonts available, and selection is by either (a) picking the picture box of the text font or (b) picking the name of the text font from the column list.

The procedure for making a text STYLE with these icons is identical to that described when making the six previous STYLES, the difference being that you can 'see' what the text

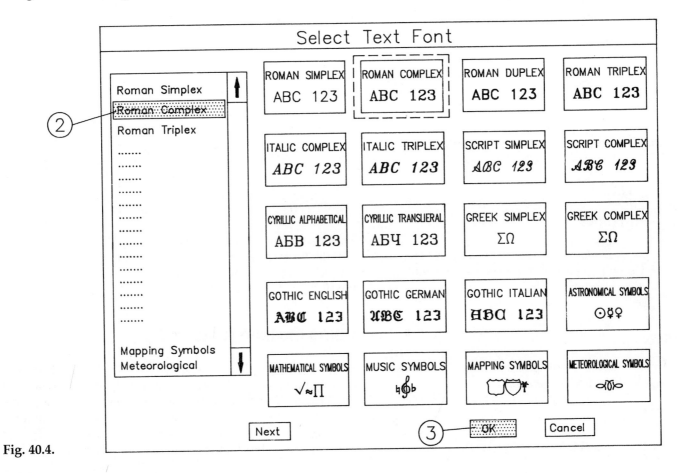

Fig. 40.4.

126 *Beginning AutoCAD*

AutoCAD AutoCAD AutoCAD *AutoCAD*
MONOTXT   ROMAN COMPLEX   GOTHIC ITALIAN   SANSSERIF OBLIQUE

SCRIPT SIMPLEX FONT
AutoCAD is a draughting package which allows the use of different text fonts.

GOTHIC GERMAN FONT
AutoCAD is a draughting package which allows the use of different text fonts.

TECHNIC FONT
AutoCAD is a draughting package which allows the use of different text fonts.

EUROROMAN FONT
AutoCAD is a draughting package which allows the use of different text fonts.

CYRILLIC FONT
АфуоВАГ ит а гсафжзуинж павкажд цзивз аллоцт узд фтд ое гиеедсдну удчу еонут.

Fig. 40.5. Different fonts.

will be like. To use the icons, refer to Fig. 40.5 and we will make four new styles using the information in Table 40.2.

Table 40.2

Icon pick	MONOTXT	ROMAN COMPLEX	GOTHIC ITALIAN	SANSSERIF OBLIQUE
Height	10	10	10	10
Width factor	1	1	1	1
Obliquing angle	0	0	0	0
Backwards	N	N	N	N
Upside-down	N	N	N	N
Vertical	N	N	N	N
DTEXT Start point	25,215	110,215	195,215	280,215

1. Select the sequence

    Draw
    Text >
    Set Style...   from the menu bar.

2. Pick the **icon box** for **ROMAN COMPLEX**, and note that the name will be highlighted in the column list in blue.
3. Pick the **OK** box.
4. The various prompts will then appear.
5. When completed use **DTEXT** with the word 'AutoCAD' using the text start positions listed above, i.e. (110,215).
6. Repeat the procedure for the other three icon fonts given.

Figure 40.5 also gives a phrase printed using six other icons.

Try these (or others) for yourself, entering different values at the prompts if you want.

To return to the default text setting, select **DTEXT** then **STYLE:** and enter the name **STANDARD**. The prompt should appear as `<Txt>` or `<Simplex>` depending on how your system was originally set up.

❑ Summary

1. FONTS defined the pattern of text characters.
2. STYLES define the parameters used to draw text.
3. STYLES can be made by the user.
4. FONTS are pre-determined by AutoCAD.
5. Note the difference when selecting 'STYLE:' and 'Style'. 'STYLE:' is used to define the text style and 'Style' is used to select an already made style.

Note

I feel that the creation of fancy text styles is a bit of a waste of time for engineering draughting. Generally engineering drawings would use one or two different types of text, and these would probably be set for the user within the standard sheet drawing. However, for artistic type work, fonts and styles do offer an unlimited source of ideas, and the user can spend hours creating different styles with the fonts available.

41. User exercise 5

Open the file of the ten squares made in User exercise 4, and copy them to two other places as shown in Fig. 41.1. We will now add text to the squares using different styles.

Create two new styles using the icon fonts as follows

    ITALIC TRIPLEX of height 10
    MONOTXT of height 5.

Now select

    DRAW
    Style
enter   **ITALICT<R>**
    centre or **FIT** as necessary for the text position
    0<R> for the rotation
    pick point in top LH box
enter   **F1<R>**
    <RETURN>

Using this STYLE, repeat the sequence for F2–F10 as shown.

Repeat the above procedure using **MONOTXT** as the style name and add the names FLIP, COORDS... as indicated.

Now create four STYLES of your own choosing and enter the various text in the other two sets of squares. The fonts used to complete Fig. 41.1 are listed for your convenience, and you can use them or experiment with some fonts of your own choice.

Dimensions and text styles

Refer to Fig. 41.2 and draw a horizontal line, a vertical line and a circle to your own sizes. Set the following **dimvar** settings from the **DIM** menu

    dimcen 0   dimtad OFF   dimtih ON
    dimtoh ON   dimtvp 0

1. Select

    DTEXT
    STYLE

AutoCAD prompts   Style name (or ?) ...
enter   **STANDARD<R>**
then   Cancel command with CTRL C

2. Dimension the three entities drawn.
3. (a) Select **DTEXT, Style** and enter **ITALICT** as the style name, then cancel the command (**CTRL C**).
    (b) Dimension the three entities.
4. Alter the text style to **ROMAND** and dimension the entities.
5. Finally alter the text style to **GREEKC** and dimension.

The dimension **text** style will be displayed as the current **DTEXt Style** irrespective of the dimension dimvar setting. This can be checked with dimtxt which will probably be set to 3.

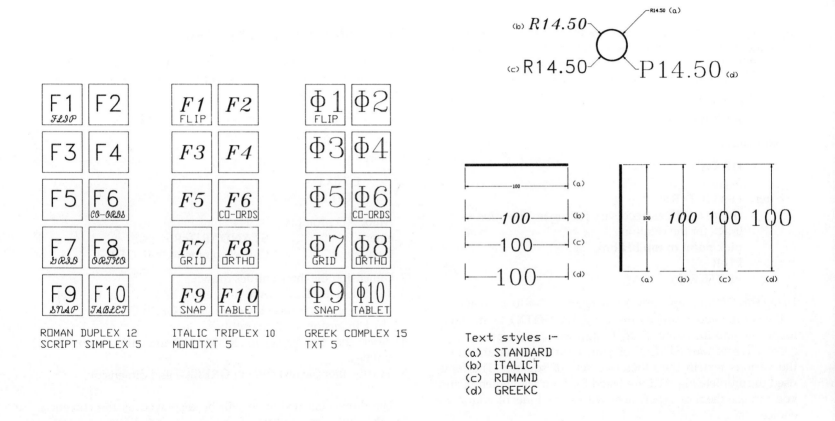

Fig. 41.1. Using different text styles (icon fonts).

Fig. 41.2. Using different text styles (icon fonts) for dimensioning.

42. BLOCKS

A block is a drawing or part of a drawing which can be 'stored away' for future use *within the drawing being worked on*. The block may be a nut, a diode, a tree or a complete drawing.

To demonstrate BLOCKS, we will edit the **WORKDRG** shape which has been used in many earlier lessons, so **Open...** the appropriate file and delete every entity but the original outline and the two circles. Then **ZOOM A**. If you do not have this drawing on disk then don't panic. Simply make a rectangular shape with two circles in it.

Creating a block

Select from the screen menu

```
BLOCKS
BLOCK:
```

AutoCAD prompts enter	Block name (or ?) **?<R>**
AutoCAD prompts enter	Block(s) to list<*> **<RETURN>**

AutoCAD responds by flipping to the text screen, with the message

```
Defined blocks
User      External    Dependent   Unnamed
Blocks    References  Blocks      Blocks
0         0           0           ?
```

i.e. we have not yet made any blocks.

Flip back to the drawing screen and repeat the **BLOCK:** command.

AutoCAD prompts enter	Block name (or ?) **BL1<R>**
AutoCAD prompts respond	Insertion base point **by picking the lower LH corner of shape** (OSNAP)
AutoCAD prompts enter	Select objects **w<R>** w – for window **window complete shape <RETURN>**

The shape will disappear as it has been made into a block and stored in memory. Now select **BLOCK:** and **?** to list the blocks which have been made. The message as above will appear with the following alterations

```
Defined blocks
BL1

User
Blocks
1
```

The rest of the message will be unaltered.

Inserting a block

To use a block which has been made, we must INSERT it into the drawing, so select from the screen menu

BLOCKS
INSERT:

AutoCAD prompts	Block name (or ?)
enter	**BL1\<R\>**
AutoCAD prompts	Insertion point (note the DRAG effect)
enter	**180,110\<R\>**
AutoCAD prompts	X scale factor\<1\>...
enter	**1 or \<RETURN\>** (to accept default, i.e. full size)
AutoCAD prompts	Y scale factor...
enter	**\<RETURN\>** (i.e. Y=X scale)
AutoCAD prompts	Rotation angle\<0.00\>
enter	**\<RETURN\>** (i.e. no rotation of block)

All going well, your block will be inserted full size into the point stated.

Now repeat the INSERT command, using BL1 as the block name with the information given in Fig. 42.1, i.e. the insertion point, X–Y scale and rotation angle.

Using erase with a block

Before proceeding, we will investigate erasing a block, so select the ERASE command and pick one of the inserted blocks. The complete block will have been erased, although it has made up of several line and circle entities. This is because a block is treated by AutoCAD as a *single entity*, which include all text, dimensions, etc. As the single entity effect can result in difficulties, AutoCAD overcomes this with (1) the EXPLODE command and (2) using *INSERT.

1. EXPLODE – select from the menu

   EDIT
   EXPLODE

   Now pick one of the blocks. It will change appearance, and when you press \<RETURN\> it will be redisplayed as if nothing has happened. Now select ERASE, and pick one of the lines/circles of this block. Only the entity selected will be erased, i.e. the EXPLODE command has 'restored' the block into its individual entities.

2. *INSERT – erase all entities from the screen, then

   BLOCKS
   INSERT:

AutoCAD prompts	Block name
enter	***BL1**
AutoCAD prompts	Insertion point
enter	**180,110\<R\>**
AutoCAD prompts	Scale factor\<1\>
enter	**\<RETURN\>** (i.e. accept default of 1)
AutoCAD prompts	Rotation angle\<0\>
enter	**\<RETURN\>**

The block will be inserted at the point (180,110). Now select ERASE then EXPLODE, and pick any entity on the block. Only that single entity should be erased, i.e. the *INSERT command has inserted the block as single entities.

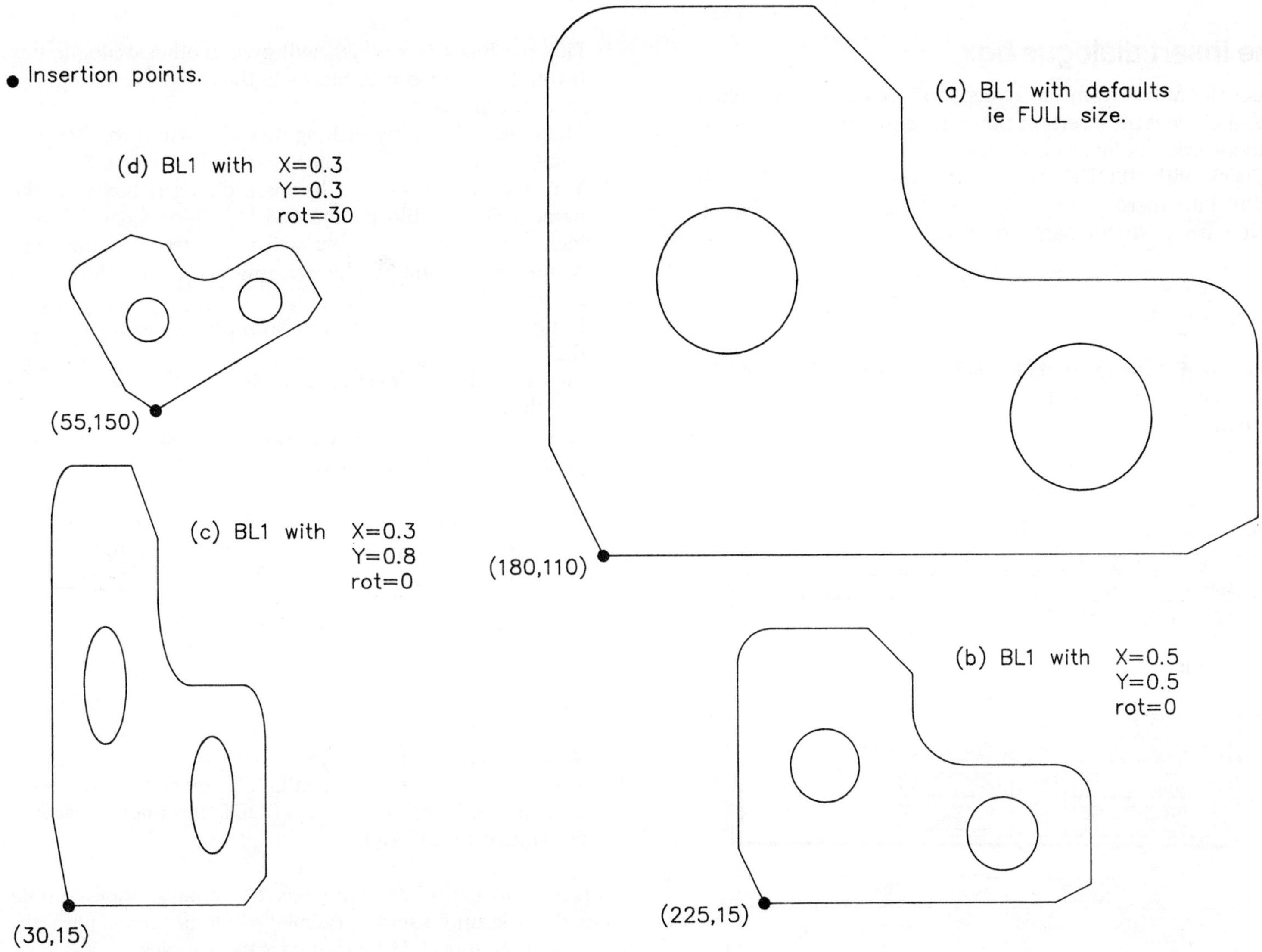

• Insertion points.

(a) BL1 with defaults ie FULL size.

(d) BL1 with X=0.3
Y=0.3
rot=30

(55,150)

(c) BL1 with X=0.3
Y=0.8
rot=0

(180,110)

(b) BL1 with X=0.5
Y=0.5
rot=0

(30,15)

(225,15)

Fig. 42.1. Inserting block BL1.

The insert dialogue box

Erase all entities from the screen, and make two new blocks: BL2, a circle with insertion point at centre and BL3, a square with insertion point at a corner.

Check with **BLOCK** then ? that the three blocks BL1, BL2 and BL3 are there.

Now use the menu bar, and select

    Draw
    Insert...

This will give the Insert dialogue box, as shown in Fig. 42.2.

We will demonstrate the use of this box with the following sequence

1. Pick the Block box which will give another dialogue box listing the defined user blocks in the current drawing, e.g. BL1, BL2 and BL3.
2. Make BL3 current by picking it, and it will turn blue. The name BL3 will appear in the Selection box. Pick OK.
3. You will be returned to the main dialogue box with the name BL3 in the Block name box.
4. Pick the OK box, and you will be returned to the command prompt line of the drawing screen, i.e. AutoCAD prompts: Insertion point.
5. Continue as before with the prompts to insert the block BL3.
6. Repeat the **Draw, Insert...** selection.
7. Use the dialogue box to make BL2 current.
8. Pick the Specify Parameters Box (i.e. the cross will disappear) and enter the following

Insertion point	Scale	Rotation
X 100	X 2	Angle 10
Y 100	Y 0.5	
Z 0	Z 1	

9. Pick the OK box.
10. You will be returned to the drawing screen, and block BL2 will have been inserted at point (100,100) to the X and Y values entered and at a rotation angle of 10°, i.e. you should have an elliptical shape.
11. The dialogue box has the EXPLODE option: (a) no cross – no EXPLODE (b) cross – EXPLODE command is active, i.e. similar to *INSERT.

Practice with this dialogue box by making some simple shaped blocks and inserting them at different points, with different scale factors and at varying rotation angles.

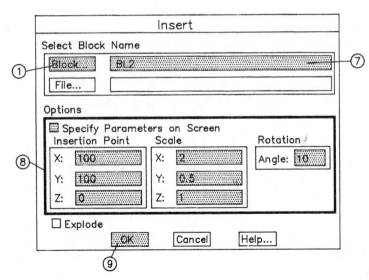

Fig. 42.2.

Block exercise

Blocks are a very useful facility with AutoCAD. We will now attempt an exercise with BLOCKS, so begin a new drawing and then draw the two shapes in Fig. 42.3. They will be used to draw Fig. 42.4.

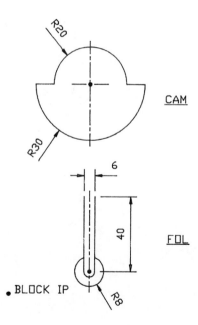

Fig. 42.3.

Making the blocks

Follow the sequence

        BLOCKS
        BLOCK:
enter   **CAM** (block name)
pick   **centre of circle** (insertion point)
enter   **w<R>**
        window the CAM shape
        <RETURN>

Repeat the above procedure for the other shape, the block name being FOL and the insertion point being as indicated. Check that these two blocks have been made with **BLOCK:** then **?**.

Inserting the CAM

To insert the CAM as shown in Fig. 42.4, enter the following

        BLOCKS
        INSERT:
enter   **CAM<R>**   for block name
enter   **80,100<R>**   for insertion point
enter   **0.5<R>**   for X scale
enter   **0.5<R>**   for Y scale
enter   **0<R>**   for rotation

The CAM will be inserted at the selected point and will have been scaled by a factor of 0.5 in the X and Y axes.

Repeat the INSERT command using the figures in Fig. 42.4 for the insertion points and rotation angles. Why not try and enter some (or all) of the variables using the dialogue box.

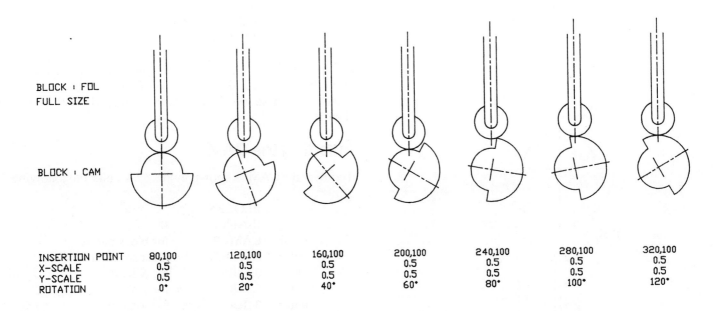

Fig. 42.4. Block exercise.

MINSERT

To insert the FOLLOWER, we will use the **MINSERT** command which allows the user to multiple insert a block in an arrayed pattern. The sequence is

BLOCKS	
MINSERT	
FOL<R>	block name
80,130<R>	insertion point
1<R>	X scale
1<R>	Y scale
0<R>	rotation
AutoCAD prompts	`Number of rows(- - -) <1>`
enter	
1<R>	
AutoCAD prompts	`Number of columns (| | |)<1>`
enter	
7<R>	
AutoCAD prompts	`Distance between columns (| | |)`
enter	
40<R>	

The follower will be arrayed as required. The followers are slightly out of position, as they are required to be touching the cams. As the distances required to be moved by the followers is not the same for each one, we will EXPLODE the inserted block, and then move each follower separately. Select **ERASE** then **EXPLODE** and pick any point on a follower.

AutoCAD prompts	`1 was minserted`

i.e. *a minserted block cannot be exploded*. This means that we will have to erase the followers and insert them individually into the positions required.

*Inserting the followers

Use the sequence below to insert the first follower at position (80,130)

BLOCKS
INSERT:
*FOL
80,130
1
0

Now complete the inserting of the rest of the followers either from the keyboard or from the dialogue box. The insertion points should be easy to work out, but in case you have problems they are (80,130); (120,130); (160,130), etc.

Finishing the drawing

The followers have to be moved onto the cams, and I will leave this for you to try yourself. Six of them are very straightforward, and one is slightly more difficult.

Activity

Tutorials 37–40 are about blocks.

❏ Summary

1. A BLOCK is a drawing which is stored away for recall.
2. A BLOCK is a single entity.
3. A BLOCK resides within the drawing in which it was created.
4. BLOCKS made are recalled with INSERT.
5. BLOCKS can be EXPLODED back to their individual entities.
6. Using INSERT *BLNAME will explode a block as it is inserted.
7. Using *INSERT only allows the BLOCK to be inserted full size.
8. A dialogue box is available with the INSERT command.

43. WBLOCKS

WBLOCKS are similar to BLOCKS in that shapes or complete drawings can be stored for future recall by the user. The difference is that while blocks are saved within the drawing in which they were made, WBLOCKS are *saved to a name directory* (in our case we will use the floppy disc) which *allows them to be accessed by any other user*. This is a very useful concept, as it allows users access to standard drawings of nuts, springs, etc. which when made once, can be made into a WBLOCK and recalled as required.

The term WBLOCK means *WORLD BLOCK*.

To use WBLOCKS we will make a title box for inserting into all our drawings. Refer to Fig. 43.1 below and use it as a guide to construct your own title box, the only limitation being in the overall sizes of the box.

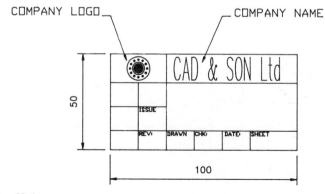

Fig. 43.1.

Making the WBLOCK

Select from the menu: BLOCKS

WBLOCK:	
AutoCAD prompts	with a dialogue box
respond	**by picking the Type It box**
AutoCAD prompts	WBLOCK file name
enter	**A:TITLE<R>**
AutoCAD prompts	Block name
enter	**<RETURN>**
AutoCAD prompts	Insertion point
respond	**by picking the lower RH corner of box**
AutoCAD prompts	Select objects
enter	**w<R>**
	window complete box
	<RETURN>

The title box will disappear as it has been made into a WBLOCK. It is in fact a separate drawing called **A:TITLE**.

Now begin a new drawing with the sequence

> **File**
> **New...**
> **B:LAYOUT**

Refer to Fig. 43.2 and make a layout of your choosing.

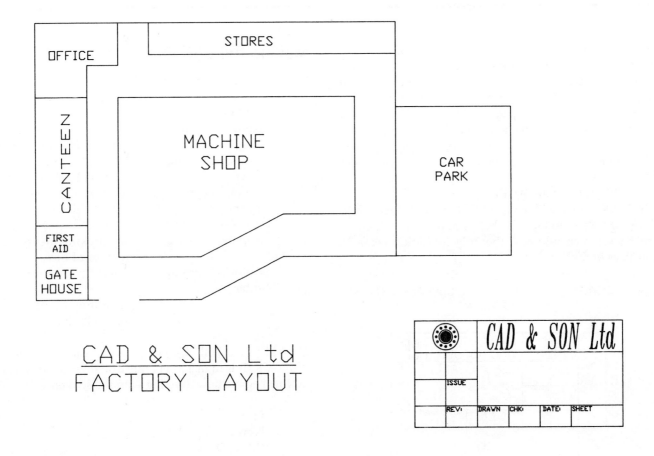

Fig. 43.2. Using WBLOCK.

Inserting the WBLOCK

To insert the title block, select

    BLOCKS
    INSERT:

AutoCAD prompts	Block name
enter	**A:TITLE\<R\>**
AutoCAD prompts	Insertion point
respond	**by picking a suitable point**
AutoCAD prompts	...as before with X,Y,rot

The title box will be inserted as required.

Notes

1. What you have achieved is to insert a drawing (remember A:TITLE is a separate drawing) into an existing drawing. This is very useful, as any drawing can be inserted as a WBLOCK into the drawing being worked on.
2. As WBLOCKS are inserted using the INSERT command, you can use the dialogue box. I will leave the user to try this on their own.
3. WBLOCKS can be stored within directories, but I feel that this is beyond the scope of this book.

Activity

Attempt Tutorial 41 which is of a simple component, and then insert your title box.

44. Attributes

An attribute is a text item which can be attached to a BLOCK or a WBLOCK. This gives the user a very powerful way of adding large amounts of repetitive text to drawings. The uses of attributes are virtually endless, but some examples are

(a) electrical circuits with all data added
(b) weld symbols containing different information
(c) parts lists containing codes, numbers off, etc.

Attributes which are added to blocks can be edited, but their main advantage is that the information can be **EXTRACTED** in a special attribute extraction file. This extracted data can then be used as input to other systems, e.g. databases, spreadsheets, word-processing packages, CNC programming, etc. The editing and extraction of attributes is beyond the scope of this book, but I will introduce the user to the concept of making attributes.

We will use Fig. 44.1 as our starting point, which is a name tag containing two pieces of information (1) a name and (2) a class code.

By referring to Fig. 44.1(a) make the name tag to the sizes given, adding the two dotted lines. These will be used as a base for our attributes.

Making the attributes

This is a simple task, but may seem involved to new users as there are several prompts which must be answered. Attributes must be **DEFINED** before they can be used, and the command for this is found in the BLOCKS option – ATTDEF, i.e. attribute definition.

Select from the screen menu

BLOCKS
ATTDEF:

AutoCAD prompts	`Inv,Con,Ver...`
enter	**\<RETURN\>**
AutoCAD prompts	`Attribute tag`
enter	**NAME** then **\<R\>**
AutoCAD prompts	`Attribute prompt`
enter	**What is the name?** then **\<R\>**
AutoCAD prompts	`Default attribute value`
enter	**ABCDEF** then **\<R\>**
AutoCAD prompts	`Justify/Style/<Start point>`
respond	select **Justify** from screen then select **center**
AutoCAD prompts	`Center point`
respond	****** MIDpoint** pick the top dotted line
AutoCAD prompts	`Height<?>`
enter	**10** then **\<R\>**
AutoCAD prompts	`Rotation angle <0>`
enter	**0** then **\<R\>**

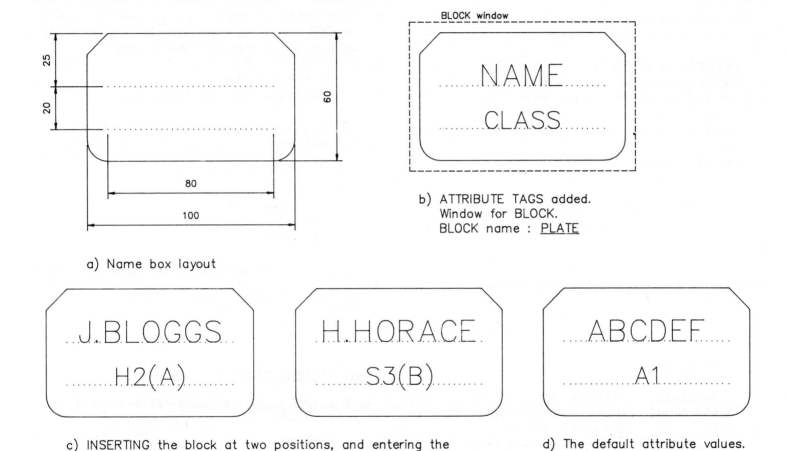

Fig. 44.1. Setting the attributes.

If all has proceeded satisfactorily, the word **NAME** will have appeared at the midpoint of the top dotted line. This is the attribute tag.

Now repeat the ATTDEF command, and enter the following in response to the various prompts

1. **<RETURN>** for Inv,Cons....
2. **CLASS<R>** at the attribute tag prompt.
3. **Enter the class<R>** at the attribute prompt line.
4. **A1<R>** as the default.
5. Select **justify, center, ****MIDpoint, pick bottom dotted line**.
6. **8<R>** for the height.
7. **0<R>** for the rotation.

The word CLASS should then be inserted at the midpoint of the bottom line, and your name tag should be as Fig. 44.1(b).

Making the block with the attributes

This is achieved in the same way as the earlier lesson on BLOCKS, so select

    BLOCKS
    BLOCK:
    A:PLATE   (for the block name)
    pick point   (pick a suitable insertion point)
    w   (for window selection)
    window complete shape with the attributes

The box and attributes will disappear as would be expected. You have now created a block containing two attributes – the NAME and the CLASS.

The ATTDIA variable

Before proceeding to the insertion of the block with the attributes, I would like to mention the system variable ATTDIA. This variable determines if a dialogue box will be used when the attributes are inserted. It has only two options

    0 – no dialogue box
    1 – dialogue box will be displayed.

At this introductory stage with attributes, I will assume that *no* dialogue box will be used, so set the variable to 0 with

           SETTINGS
           next
           SETVAR:
enter   **ATTDIA<R>**
enter   **0<R>**

The user can use the dialogue box setting of 1, however, if they want. The dialogue box is very simple to use, and should not present any problems at this stage if any user wants to set the ATTDIA value to 1.

Inserting the attribute block

This is the same procedure as used with block insertion, so

    BLOCKS
    INSERT:
    PLATE   as the block name
    pick point   for insertion point
    <R>,<R>,<R> X,Y,Rot prompts

AutoCAD prompts	Enter attribute values
	Enter the class <A1>
enter	**H2(A)<R>**
AutoCAD prompts	What is the name?
enter	**J.BLOGGS<R>**

The two attributes will be inserted in the correct place in the name tag as shown in Fig. 44.1(c). Now repeat the insert command and produce a few name plates of your own.

You can also use the **Insert...** command from the menu bar, the method being the same as that described in the BLOCK section.

Also shown in Fig. 44.1(d) is the name tag with the defaults.

❑ Summary

1. ATTRIBUTES allow text to be added to BLOCKS. This can only then be used in the current drawing.
2. ATTRIBUTES allow text to be added to WBLOCKS. This allows the attribute block to be accessed with every drawing.
3. Attributes are entered with the INSERT command either: (a) at the prompt line (ATTDIA 0) or (b) using a dialogue box (ATTDIA 1).
4. Attributes can be editing and extracted.

Attribute example

The following example is quite involved, but is very useful. I would suggest that the user tries it, as it will give some satisfaction when it is completed.

We are going to make a parts list which will contain attributes and can then be used in any future drawing, as it will be made into a WBLOCK. As we have already made a title box (**A:TITLE**) we will modify and add the parts list to it, so refer to Fig. 44.2.

The steps in this procedure are as detailed below:

1. Open a new file, A:?????=A:STDA3.
2. Insert your original **A:TITLE** block as Fig. 44.2(a)
3. Modify this title box, by adding the extra line on top. Use text to suit. This addition to the title box is the basis of the parts list, giving the item number, description, etc., i.e. the 'headings'(Fig. 44.2b).
4. Make a WBLOCK of this modified box, the name being **A:TITLEPL**.
5. Now draw the parts list layout to the sizes in Fig.44.2(c).
6. Use the ATTDEF command to make four attributes using the data supplied in Fig.44.2(d). The attribute position is shown in Fig. 44.2(e) which also shows the layout when the TAGS are added. Don't worry if the tags appear to 'run into one another'.
7. Now WBLOCK this parts list layout with the four attributes, using the name **A:PLIST** as Fig. 44.2(f).
8. Use the INSERT command with the WBLOCK name **A:PLIST** as a trial and try to complete the parts list given in Fig. 44.2(g).

If you have been successful, you now have a WBLOCK which contains attribute information relating to parts lists. This can then be used with every drawing in future.

There have now been three WBLOCKS made

1. **A:TITLE** – the original title box.
2. **A:TITLEPL** – a modified title box, containing an extra 'line'.
3. **A:PLIST** – a parts list containing four attributes.

Now refer to Fig. 44.3 and

1. Make the component to the sizes given (not too important).
2. Insert the WBLOCK **A:TITLEPL** at a suitable point.
3. Insert the WBLOCK **A:PLIST** 'on top' of the title box.
4. Add the attributes as the prompts appear.
5. All being well, your parts list will appear as that shown in the figure.

a) ORIGINAL TITLE BOX.

b) MODIFIED TITLE BOX.

c) PARTS LIST BOX SIZES.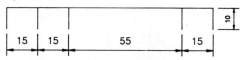

WBLOCK name : A: TITLEPL

d) ATTRIBUTE INFORMATION

TAG	PROMPT	DEF	HT,ROT
ITEM	Enter the item number	99	5,0
CODE	Enter the part code	ABC	5,0
DESC	Enter description of part	WXYZ	5,0
QTY	Enter the number off	9	5,0

e) Parts list with attribute tags and their positions.

c — or centre justify
s — for left justify

f) WBLOCK details for parts list.

WBLOCK name — A: PLIST

g) Inserting the WBLOCK — PLIST with attributes added.

3	P4	BRACKET	5
2	P3	BEARING	3
1	P2	BUSH	2

Fig. 44.2. Attribute example: (1) making the modified title box, (2) adding the attributes and (3) making the WBLOCK for the parts list.

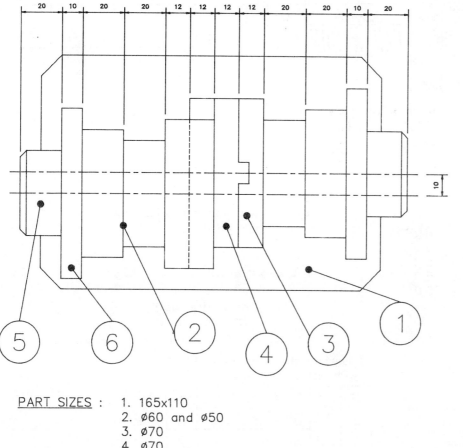

PART SIZES :   1. 165x110
                2. Ø60 and Ø50
                3. Ø70
                4. Ø70
                5. Ø40
                6. Ø80

Fig. 44.3. Attribute example: (1) draw the component as shown, (2) insert the TITLEPL WBLOCK and (3) insert the PLIST WBLOCK, and add the attributes.

45. Engineering drawings

There are many different types of drawings used in engineering, and three which we will consider are

1. Parts drawings.
2. Assembly drawings.
3. Section detail drawings.

Parts drawings

Parts drawings are generally used for the manufacture of a wide range of components. These may be one-offs, or multi-parts for use in assemblies. They usually convey information about sizes, tolerances, machined surfaces, etc. which allow the production of the parts.

There are no real rules about parts drawings, other than to ensure that the drawing is clear and well spaced out, and that all relevant information has been included.

Assembly drawings

These are usually made from parts drawings to give an indication of the completed assembly. They can also give additional information that the parts drawings cannot.

Again there are no real 'rules' about assembly drawings, other than to ensure that the parts 'mate' in the correct alignment, e.g. centre lines, bearing edges, etc. With AutoCAD, the TRIM and REDRAW commands will be used extensively, and care must be taken to ensure that lines which 'overlap' when parts are moved together are erased.

Detail drawings

These drawings are used to detail certain components. They may form part of an existing drawing, or be a separate drawing. Again there are no rules. The user simple works on one part of the drawing, and then proceeds to another part. The ZOOM command is of considerable advantage with detail drawings.

Activity

I have included one type of each drawing for the user to attempt. Tutorial 42 gives a simple parts drawing of a pulley arrangement which consists of four different components. Tutorial 43 is a sectional assembly drawing of the pulley, using the parts from the previous tutorial. Tutorial 44 is a detailed drawing of a different pulley.

46. Using the SETUP command

The most common question I am asked about AutoCAD is 'how do you set your scale'. Ideally everyone should draw full-size drawings, and plot them as required, but traditional draughtsmen seem to find this concept difficult to accept. Before Release 12, AutoCAD had a SETUP command available for selection from the on screen menu. This command allowed the user to set the scale for the size of paper being used. The command is still available in Release 12 but it requires a few menu selections before it can be activated. To illustrate its use, we will draw one large scale and one small scale drawing.

Large scale drawing

Start a new drawing, but *do not* enter your standard sheet name. Select the following sequence from the menu bar

> **View**
> **Layout >**
> **MV Setup**

AutoCAD prompts	`Initialising...`
then	`MVSETUP loaded`
	`...`
	`...Enable paper/Model Space <Y>`
enter	**N<R>**
AutoCAD prompts	`TILEMODE...Release 10 setup`
then	`Select the Units from the screen menu`
select	**metric**
AutoCAD prompts	`Select the Scale from the screen menu`
select	**1:1000**
AutoCAD prompts	`Select the paper size from the screen menu`
select	**420×297**

AutoCAD will reply with a border. At the command line, enter LIMITS and observe that they are (0,0) and (420000,297000). What we have set up is an A3 sized paper on which we are going to draw at 1000 times normal size.

Refer to Fig. 46.1(a) and set the GRID to 10000 and the SNAP to 5000, then use the LINE command to draw the house outline to the sizes given, e.g. LINE to point @250000,0, etc.

Complete the house, designing your own door and windows and select a suitable hatch pattern for the roof. The one shown is AR-RSHKE at a scale pattern of 30.

Small scale drawing

Begin a new drawing as before, then use the **View** procedure described above with the following settings: units – metric; scale – other and enter 0.01; and paper – 420×297. Now enter LIMITS and observe that they are (0,0) to (4.2,2.97), i.e. an A3 sized paper on which will be a 1/100 scaled drawing.

Refer to Fig. 46.1(b) and set the GRID to 0.1 and the SNAP to 0.05 and draw the component given. Try and add the correct sized text.

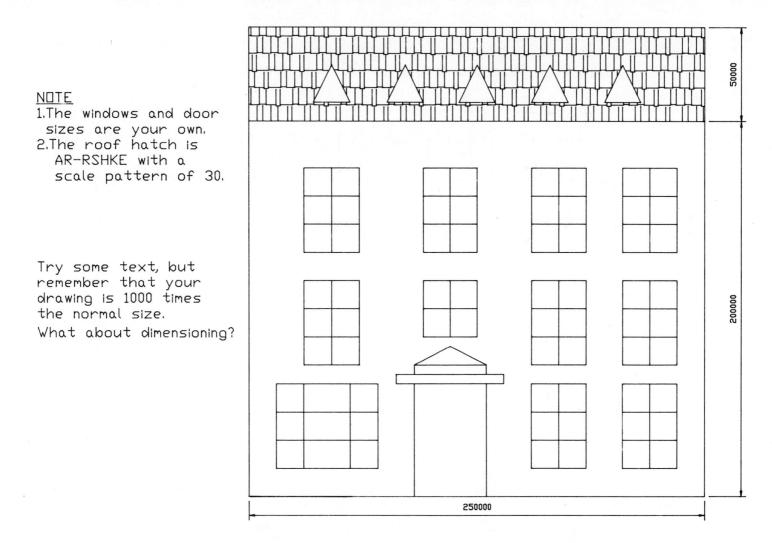

Fig. 46.1(a). Using the MVSETUP for a large drawing.

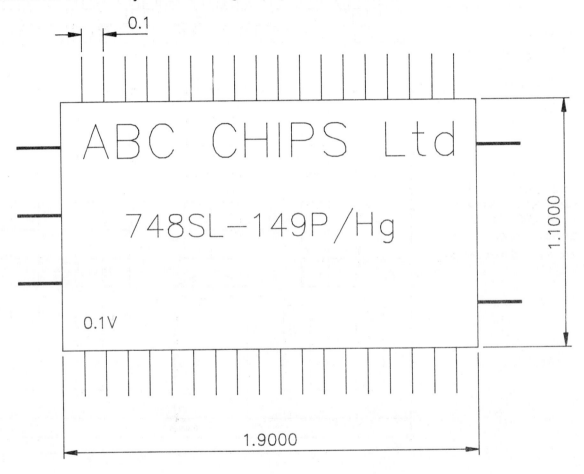

Fig. 46.1(b). Using MVSETUP for a small drawing.

47. Point filters

Point filters are the .x, .y, .z, .xy, .xz and .yz which the reader will have noticed on the **LINE** screen menu. They allow the user to access coordinate information from points already drawn on the screen. We will demonstrate point filters with a worked example, so refer to Fig. 47.1 which displays a shaped block: (a) in isometric view (b) as a plan and end view in first angle projection.

Point filters will allow us to draw the front view, so open your **A:STDA3** standard sheet and draw the two views using the dimensions given. Do not add these dimensions. The points (a), (b), etc. are for reference in the command sequence which follows. Set the SNAP to OFF, and then select

> **SETTINGS**
> **next**
> **OSNAP:**

AutoCAD prompts   Object snap modes
respond   **pick INTersec then\<R\>**

Now activate the LINE command and

AutoCAD prompts   From point
respond   **pick .x**
AutoCAD   .x of
respond   **pick point a**
AutoCAD prompts   (need YZ)
respond   **pick .yz**
AutoCAD prompts   .yz of
respond   **pick point p** (note snap point on screen)

AutoCAD prompts   To point
respond   **pick .x**
AutoCAD prompts   .x of
respond   **pick point b**
AutoCAD prompts   (need YZ)
respond   **pick .yz**
AutoCAD prompts   .yz of
respond   **pick point p** (and line 1 should be drawn)

Now complete the following selections

(a) .x then point b, .yz then point q (line 2)
(b) .x then point c, .yz then point q (line 3)
(c) .x then point c, .yz then point p (line 4)
(d) .x then point d, .yz then point p (line 5)
(e) .x then point d, .yz then point r (line 6)
(f) .x then point a, .yz then point r (line 7)
(g) .x then point a, .yz then point p (line 8)
(h) \<RETURN\> to end LINE sequence.

To complete the front view, select the LINE command, then

(a) .x then point e, .yz then point r
(b) .x then point f, .yz then point s (line 9)
(c) \<RETURN\> to end sequence and complete the front view.

Point filters allow the user an additional method for drawing entities from existing objects on the screen. It is only with practice that the reader will become proficient at using them.

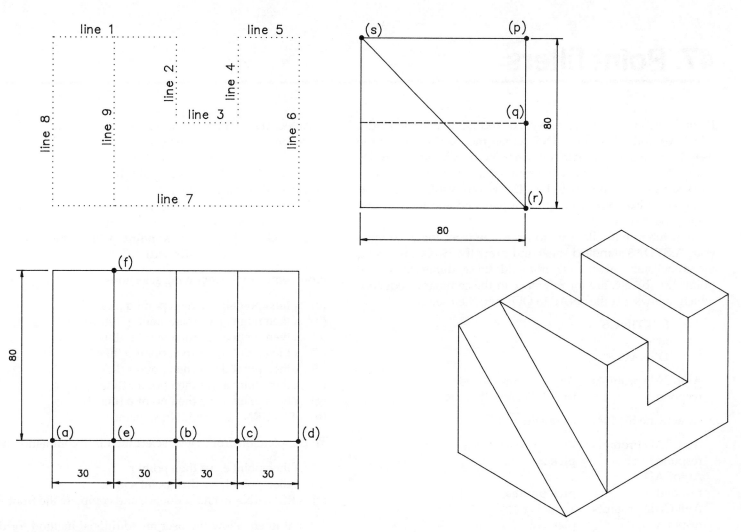

Fig. 47.1. POINT FILTER example.

154 *Beginning AutoCAD*

Tutorial 2. Draw the templates to the sizes given. Start points:
A (30,30), B (165,190), C (300,135).

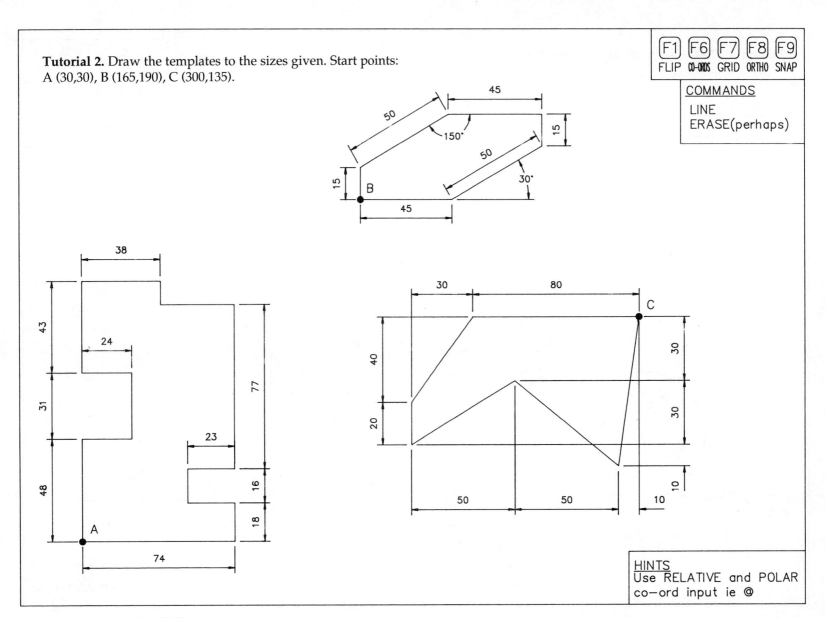

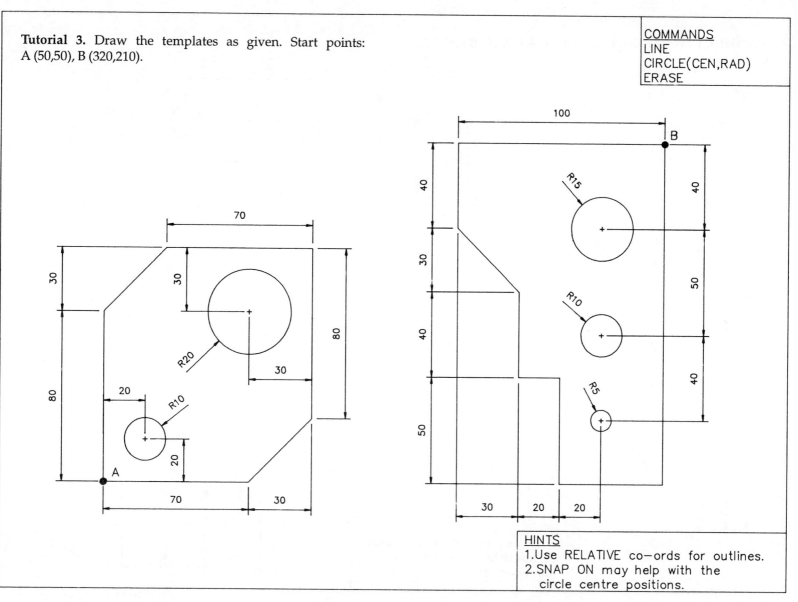

Tutorial 4. Draw the shapes as shown. A (40,30), B (180,220), C (280,45).

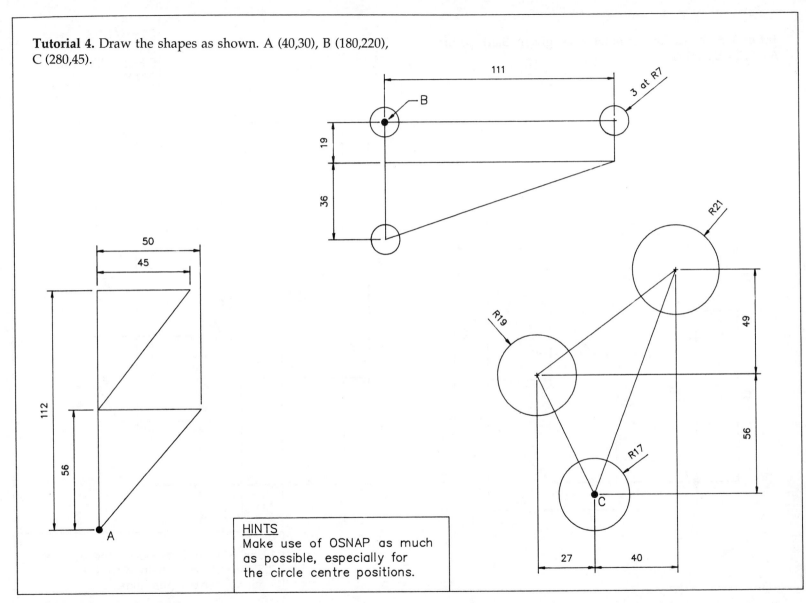

HINTS
Make use of OSNAP as much as possible, especially for the circle centre positions.

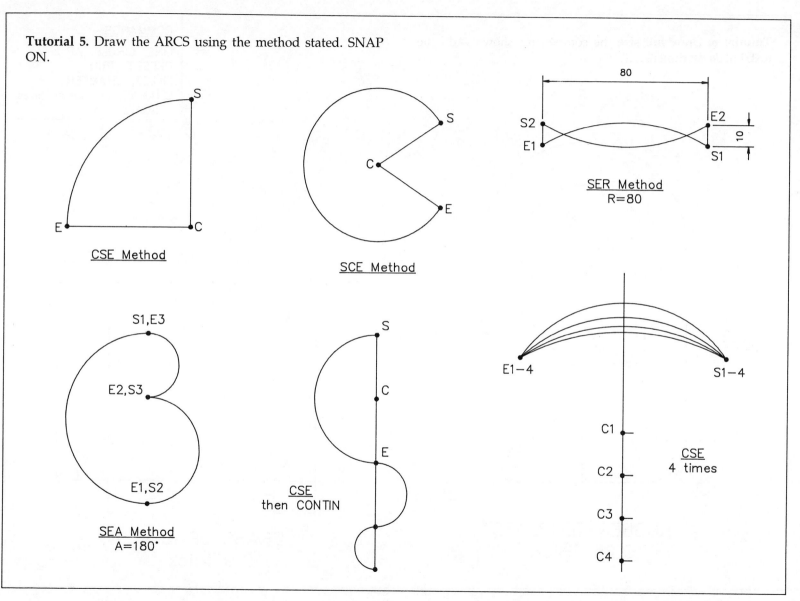

Tutorial 6. Draw full size the components shown. Add the text, but *do not* dimension.

COMMANDS
LINE, CIRCLE, ARC
OFFSET, TRIM
FILLET, CHAMFER
CHANGE for centre lines
LTSCALE 0.3

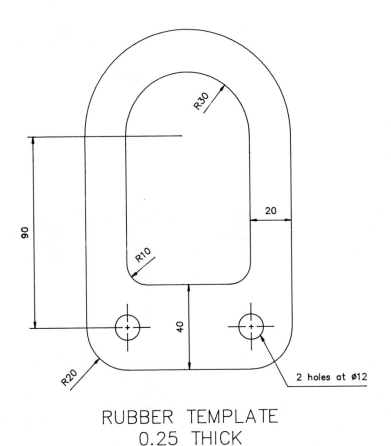

RUBBER TEMPLATE
0.25 THICK

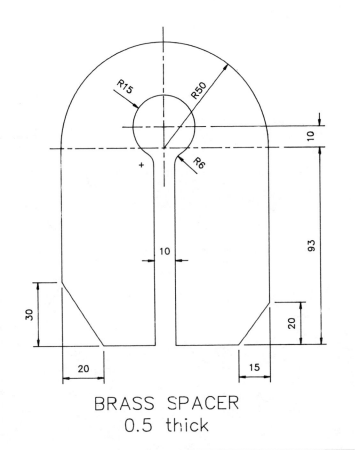

BRASS SPACER
0.5 thick

160　*Beginning AutoCAD*

Tutorial 7. Draw full size the two components. Use the OFFSET command to help with the positioning of the circle centres. Add the text.

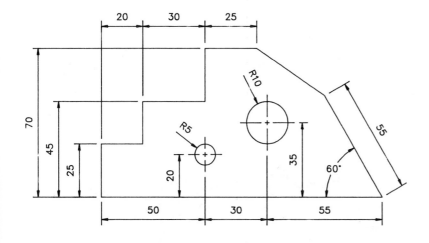

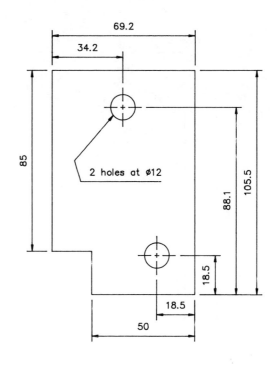

Tutorial 8. Draw as shown. Make use of OFFSET and TRIM.

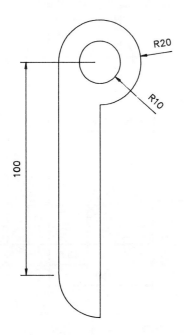

BRASS CIRCLIP

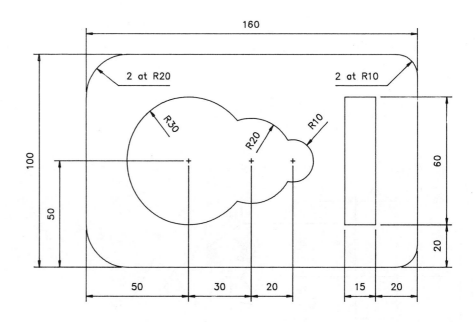

PLASTIC NAME TAG

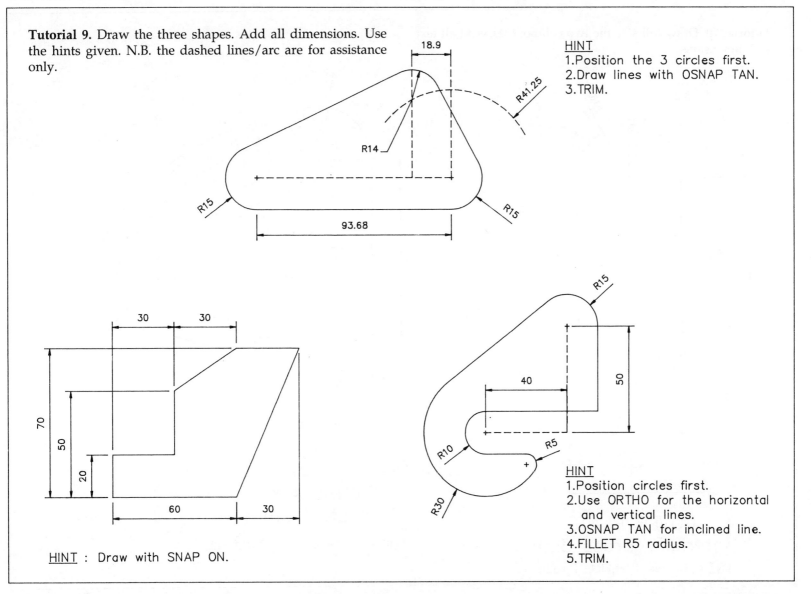

Tutorial 10. Draw full size the two components. Add all text and dimensions.

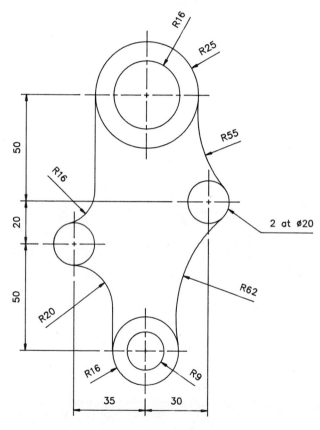

COVER PLATE
Material : Brass 3mm
HINT : Circles first, FILLET radii.

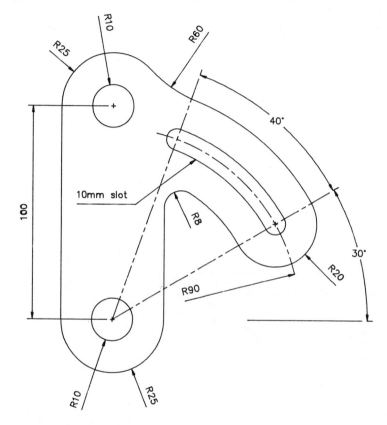

SIGNAL ARM
Mild Steel 5mm

HINT : Use OFFSET, TRIM, FILLET.

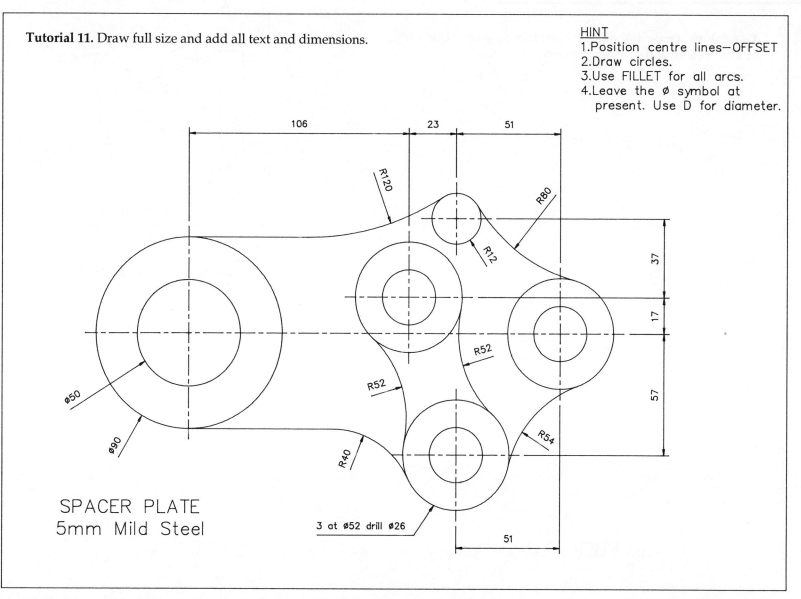

Tutorial 12. Draw the quarter template as given. Use the MIRROR command to obtain the complete outline.

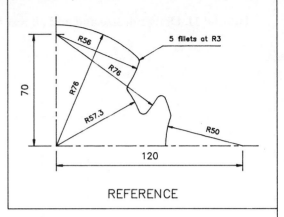

REFERENCE

HINT
1. Position lines.
2. Draw circles to given radii.
3. TRIM as required.
4. Add fillets.

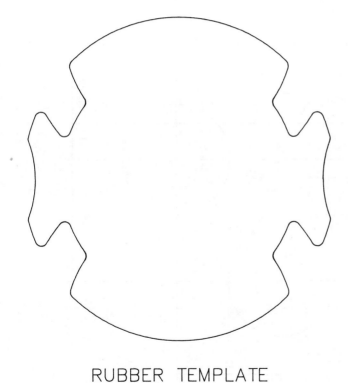

RUBBER TEMPLATE

Tutorial 13. Draw the two GATES given. Use the COPY to complete the circuit.

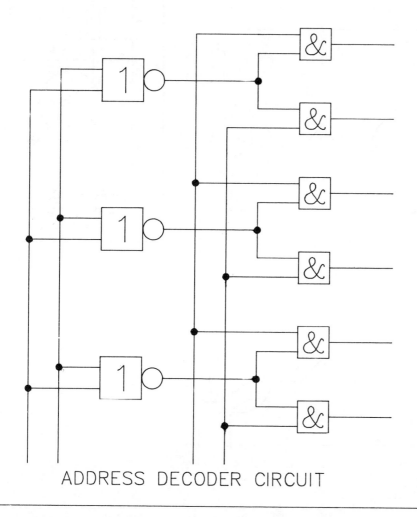

ADDRESS DECODER CIRCUIT

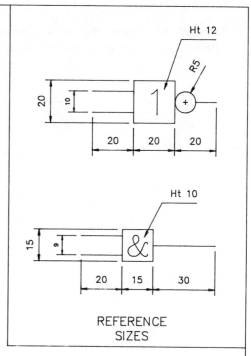

REFERENCE SIZES

HINTS
1. ORTHO, EXTEND may help.
2. Connectors are DONUTS with ID=0 and OD=3.

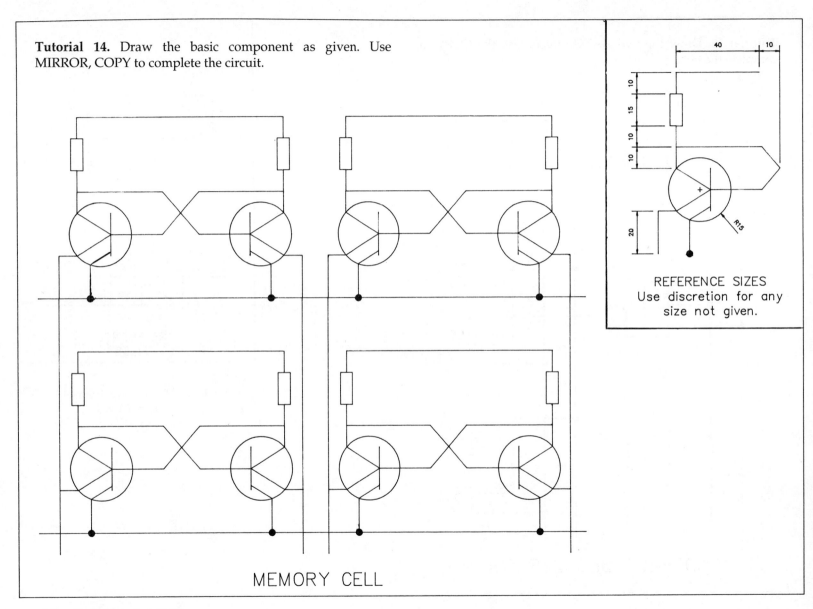

Tutorial 15. Draw the design patterns. Snap on 5 or 10.

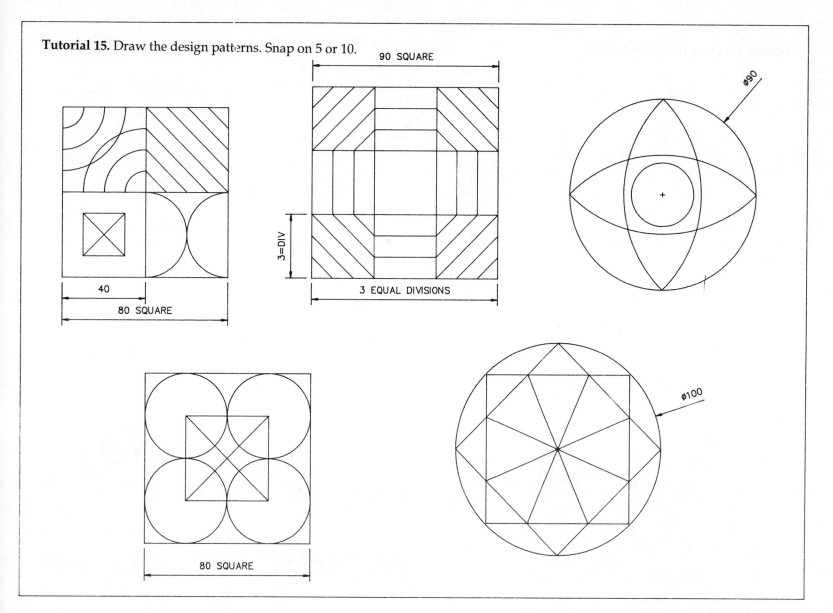

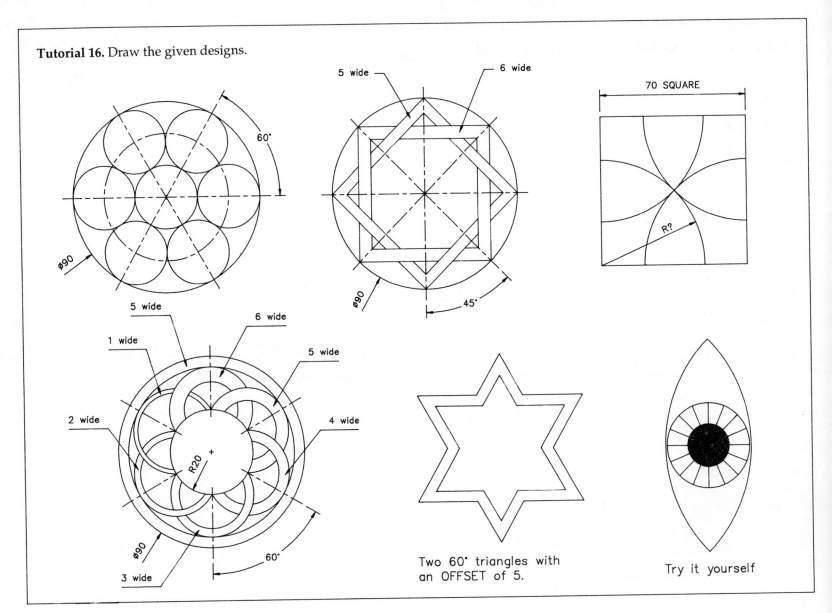

Tutorial 17. Draw full size the three views. Add *all* text and dimensions. Use appropriate layers

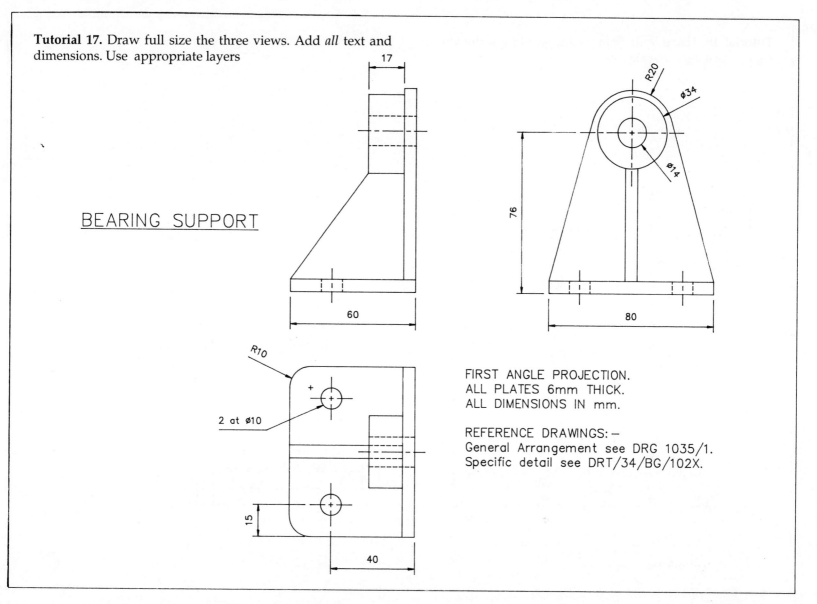

Tutorial 18. Using your floppy disk, produce a drawing as shown. Use the correct layers.

Use discretion for the sizes.

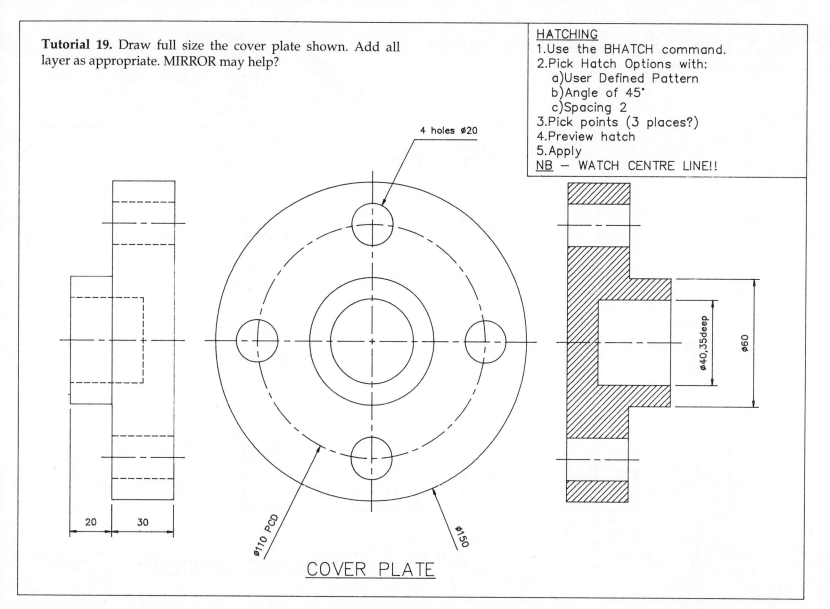

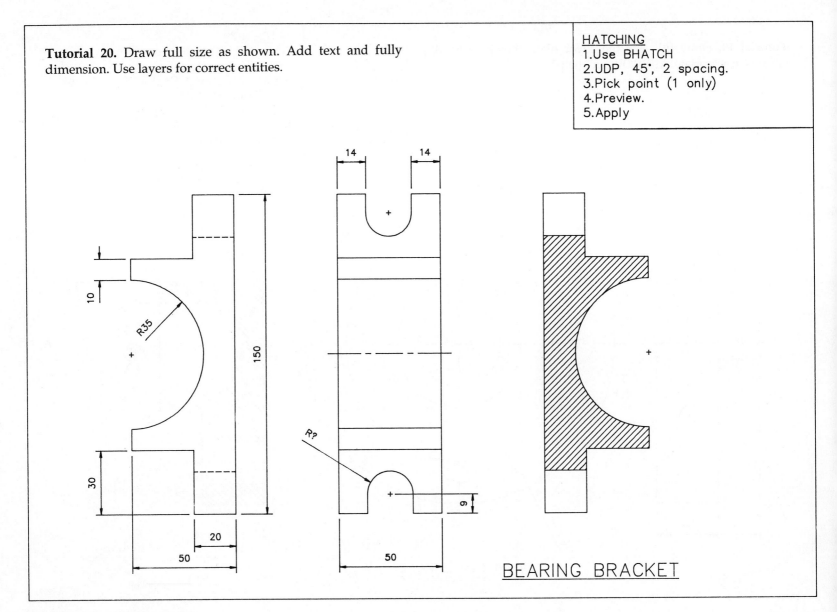

Tutorial 21. Draw full size the given views, but make the top view a section as shown in inset. Use proper layers.

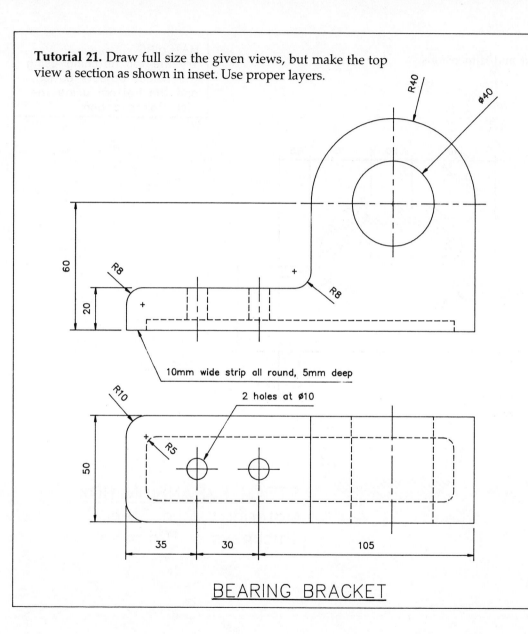

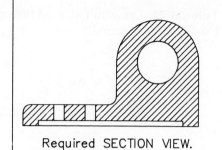

Required SECTION VIEW.

HATCHING
1. Use BHATCH
2. UDF,45,2
3. Pick points.
4. Watch the circle!!!

BEARING BRACKET

Tutorial 22. Draw full size adding all text and dimensions.
Use layers as required.

> **HATCHING**
> Try the top hatching using the Select Objects option, and the bottom using the Pick Points option.

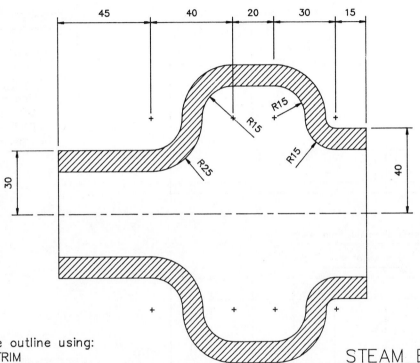

SUGGESTIONS
1. Draw the outside outline using:
   a) Circles then TRIM
   b) TTR?
   c) FILLET radii to suit.
2. OFFSET outside outline for the inside outline.
3. MIRROR the top to bottom, but do not mirror the hatching. WHY?

STEAM EXPANSION BOX
Material : Mild Steel
Thickness : 10mm

176 *Beginning AutoCAD*

Tutorial 23. Draw full size, adding all text and dimensions. Use layers.

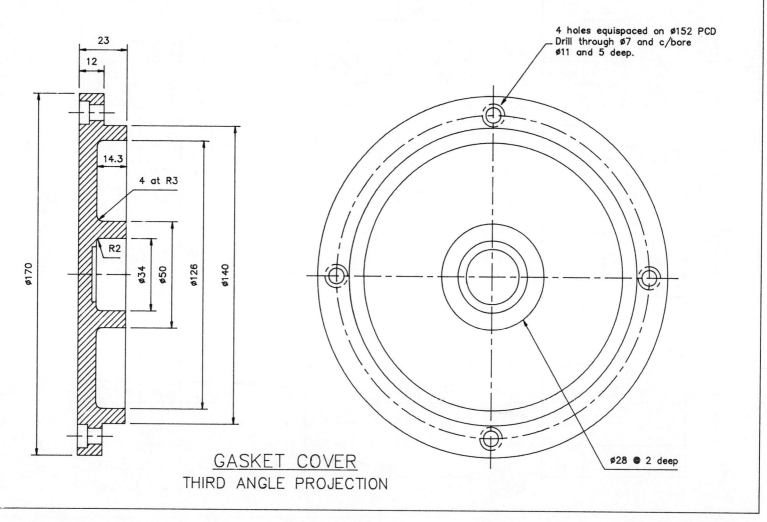

GASKET COVER
THIRD ANGLE PROJECTION

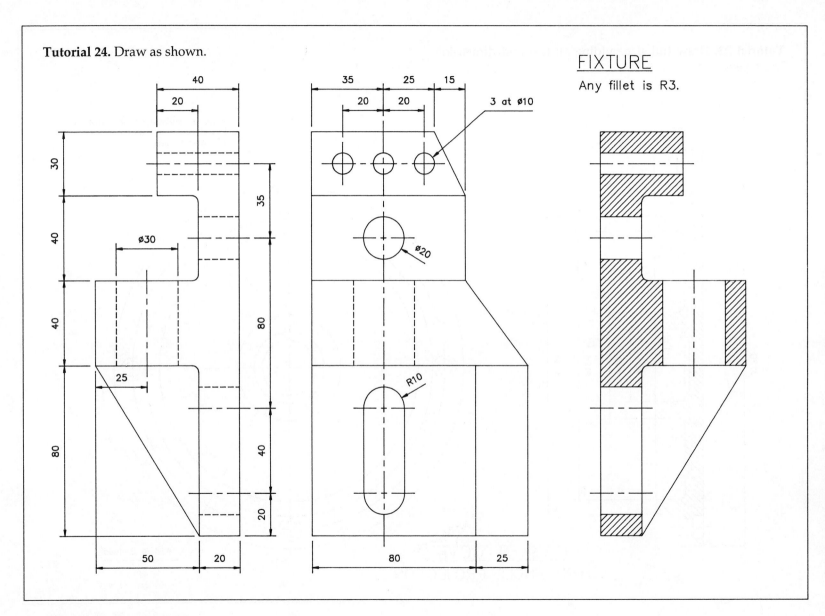

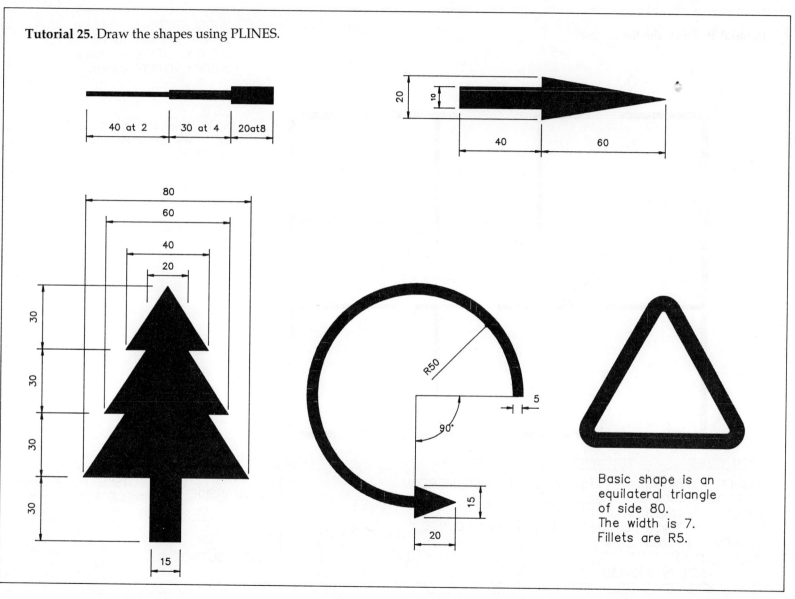

Tutorial 26. Draw the flat as given.

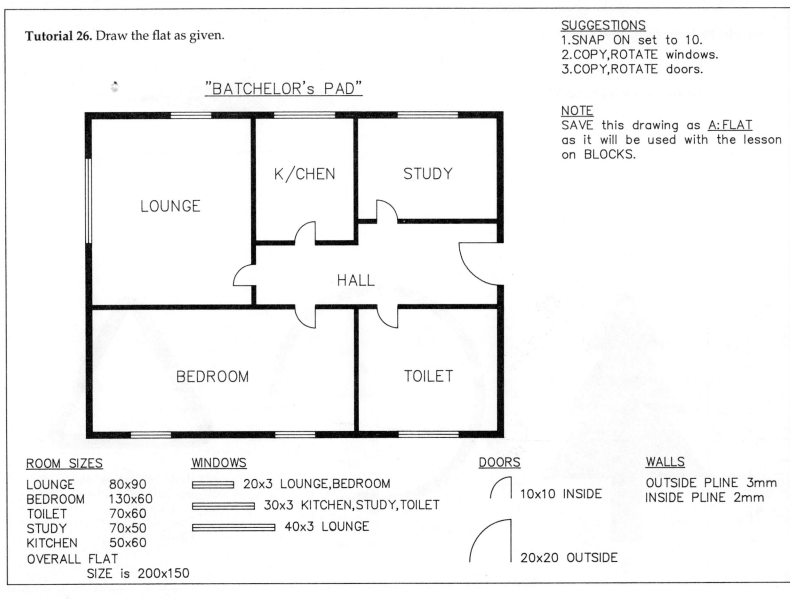

Tutorial 27. Draw and add all text and dimensions.

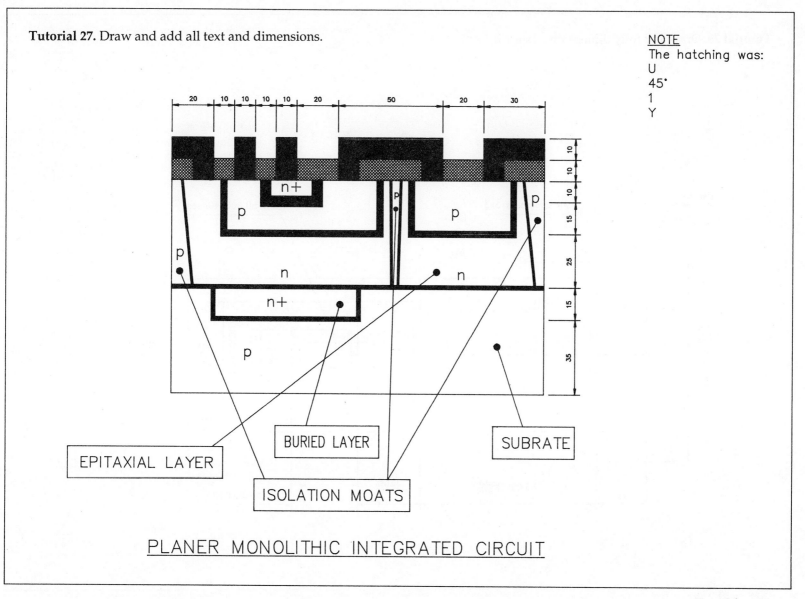

Tutorial 28. Draw and fully dimension as shown.

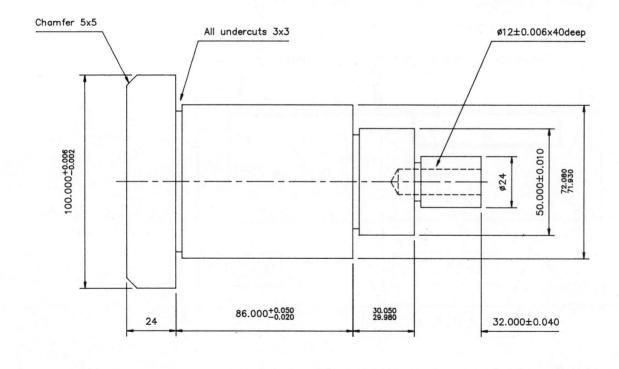

182 *Beginning AutoCAD*

Tutorial 29. Draw the designs using the ARRAY command with the information given.

POLAR
10 items
Outside radius 50
Inside radius 40

RECTANGULAR
5 ROWS, 4 COLUMNS
Row distance 20
Column distance 20

RECTANGULAR 4 ROWS, 5 COLUMNS
Row distance 10, Column distance 30

OD 20, ID 10
OD 10, ID 8
DONUTS

BASIC SIZES

Tutorial

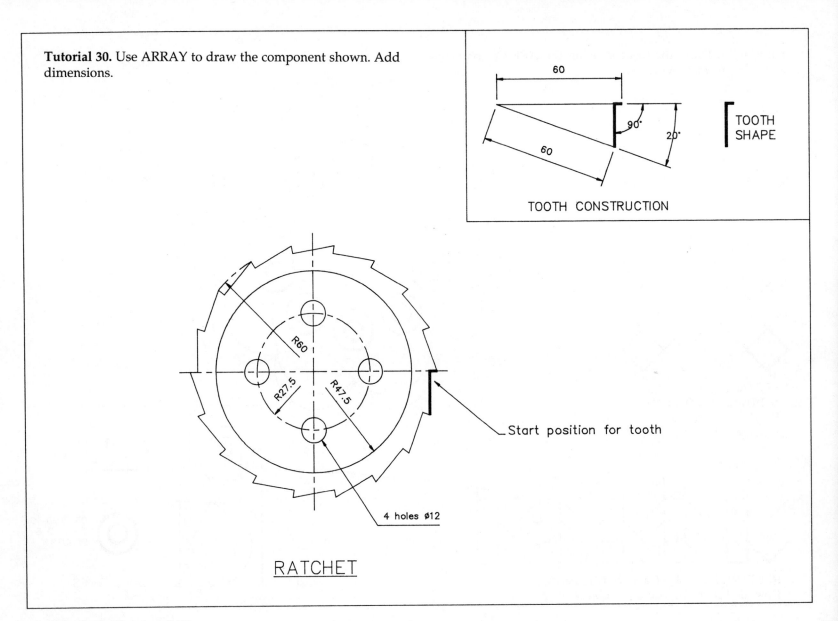

Tutorial 31. Draw and fully dimension. Use ARRAY for (a) holes, (b) slots.

COVER PLATE

SECTION AA

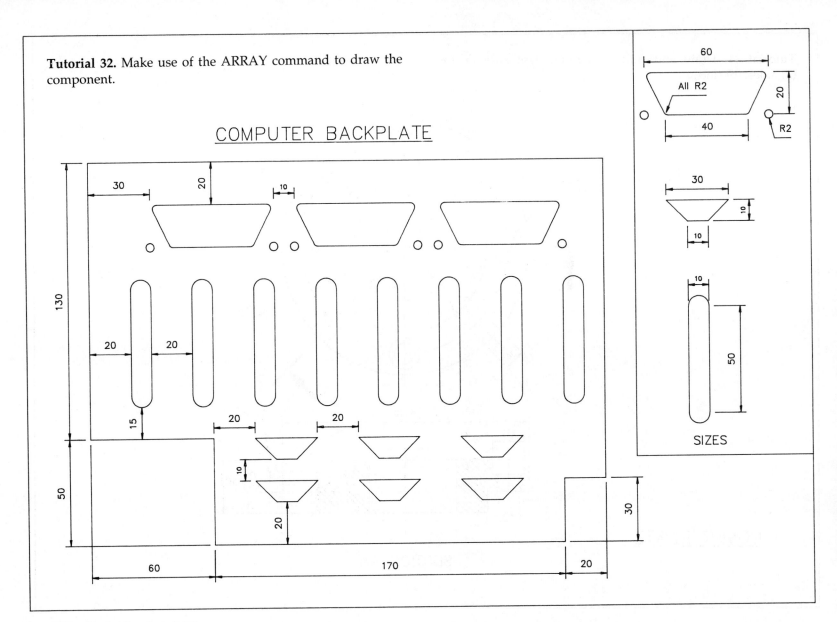

Tutorial 33. (1) Draw the bulb outline to the sizes given. (2) Scale the bulb by 1/4. (3) Use ARRAY to create the pattern given. (4) As an added extra, dimension the bulb.

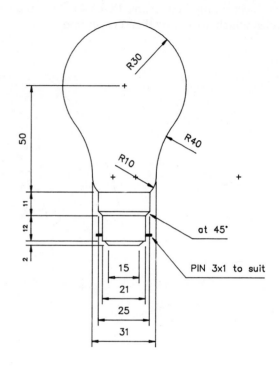

BASIC BULB SIZES

BOBMAX
240V   60W

NOTES
1. The bulb outline is tricky to draw, and will require some thought, especially with the R10 positioning.
2. The ARRAY centre is at your discretion.

Tutorial 187

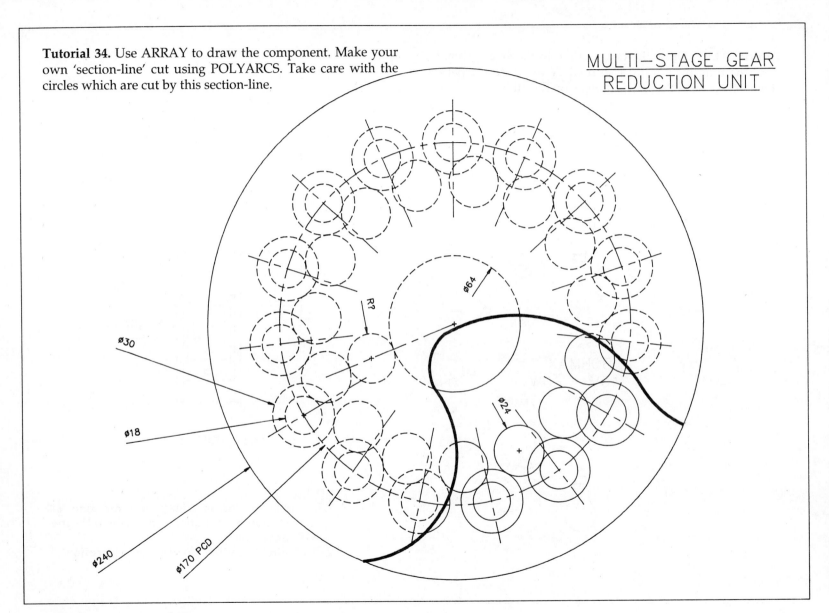

Tutorial 35. Using the data supplied, draw the two given views. Note: the BREAK command may be useful with the triangular plate.

GEAR DETAILS

A. INTERNAL GEAR
OD=140mm
ID=120mm
Depth=40mm
Thickness=10mm

B. INPUT SHAFT
Gear dia=60mm
Shaft dia=10mm
Thickness=12mm

C. IDLER
Gear dia=30mm
Shaft dia=10mm
PCD=90mm
Thickness=12mm

D. OUTPUT MEMBER
Triangular plate of 20mm thickness, the end radii made to suit.

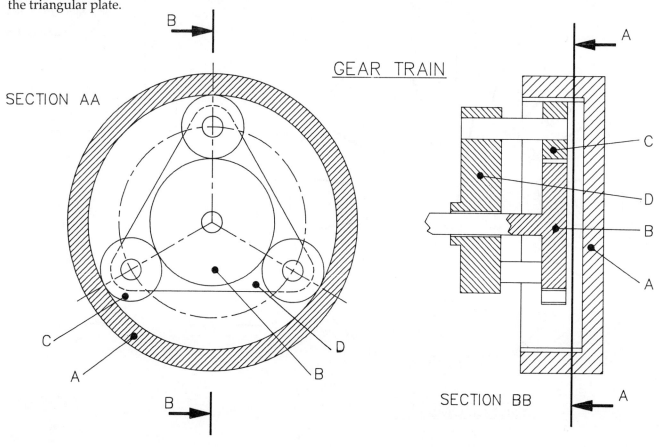

GEAR TRAIN

SECTION AA

SECTION BB

Tutorial 189

Tutorial 36. Use the ARRAY/CHANGE method to draw the speedometer shown. Try the text at the bottom using a similar procedure.

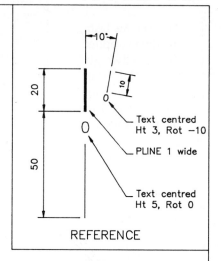

REFERENCE

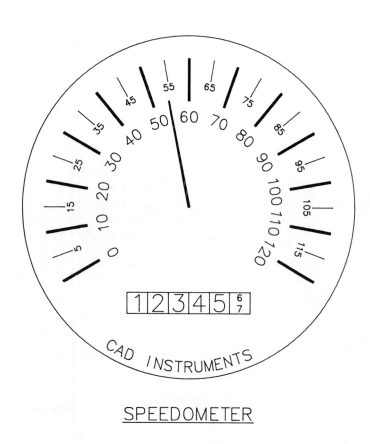

SPEEDOMETER

Tutorial 37. Make the four blocks using the sizes and names given, and use them to create a design of your choice.

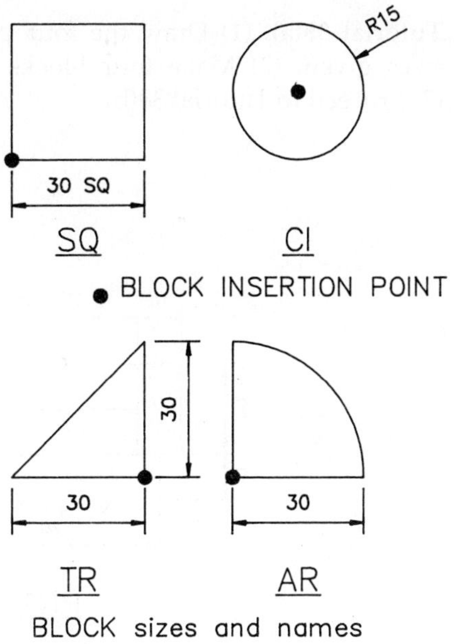

30 SQ

SQ CI

• BLOCK INSERTION POINT

30

30 30

TR AR

BLOCK sizes and names

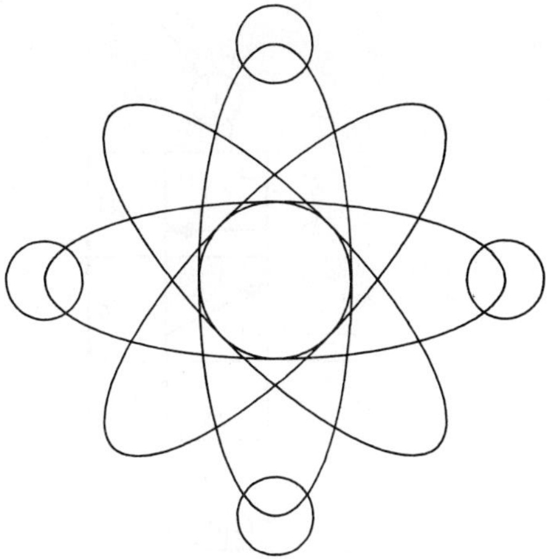

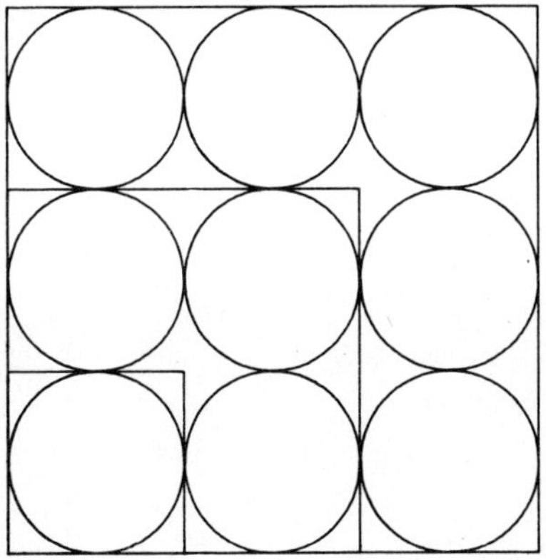

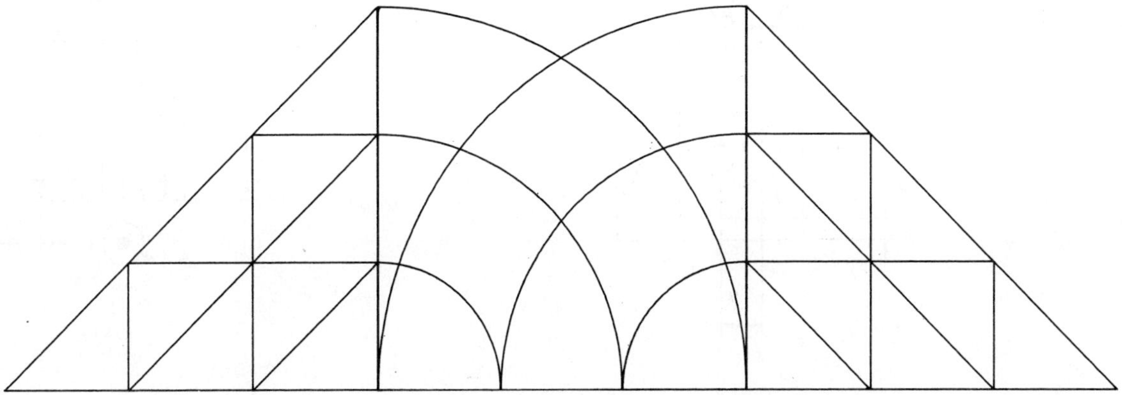

R15

Tutorial 191

Tutorial 38(a). (1) Draw the four pneumatic symbols to the sizes given. (2) Make four blocks using the stated names. (3) Proceed to Tutorial 38(b).

NB: 1. Sizes are not all given. Use your discretion as required.
2. Select a suitable block insertion point.

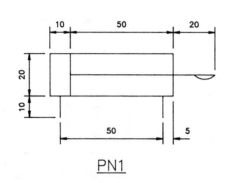

PN1

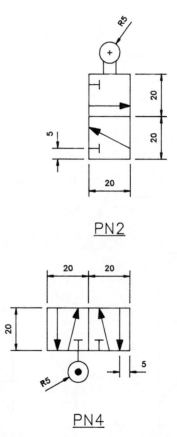

PN2

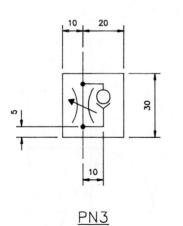

PN3

PN4

192 *Beginning AutoCAD*

Tutorial 38(b). Use the blocks created in Tutorial 38(a) to complete the pneumatic circuit. N.B. (1) the *XY* scale is 0.75. (2) ORTHO for HIDDEN lines.

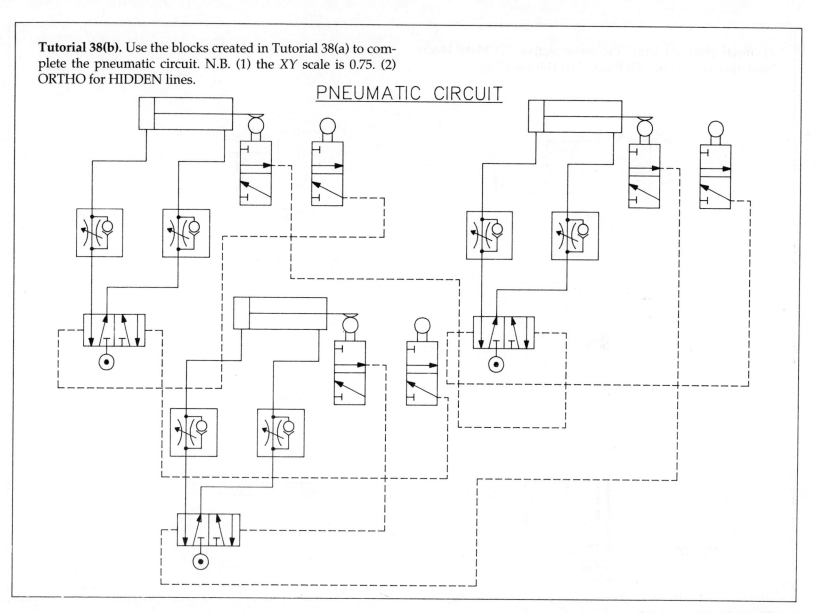

PNEUMATIC CIRCUIT

Tutorial 39(a). (1) Draw the seven shapes. (2) Make blocks with the given names. (3) Proceed to Tutorial 39(b).

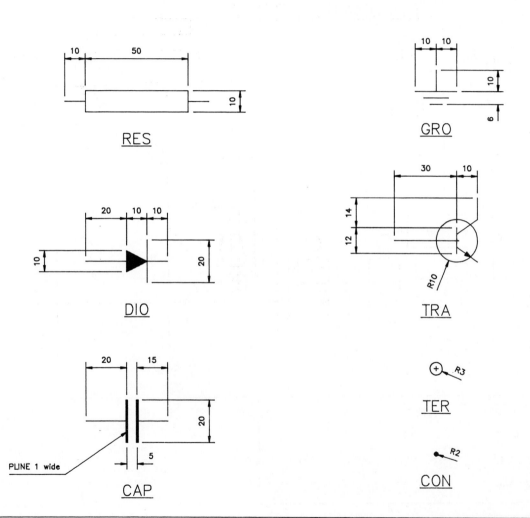

Tutorial 39(b). Use all the blocks from Tutorial 39(a) to complete the circuit. Add all text.

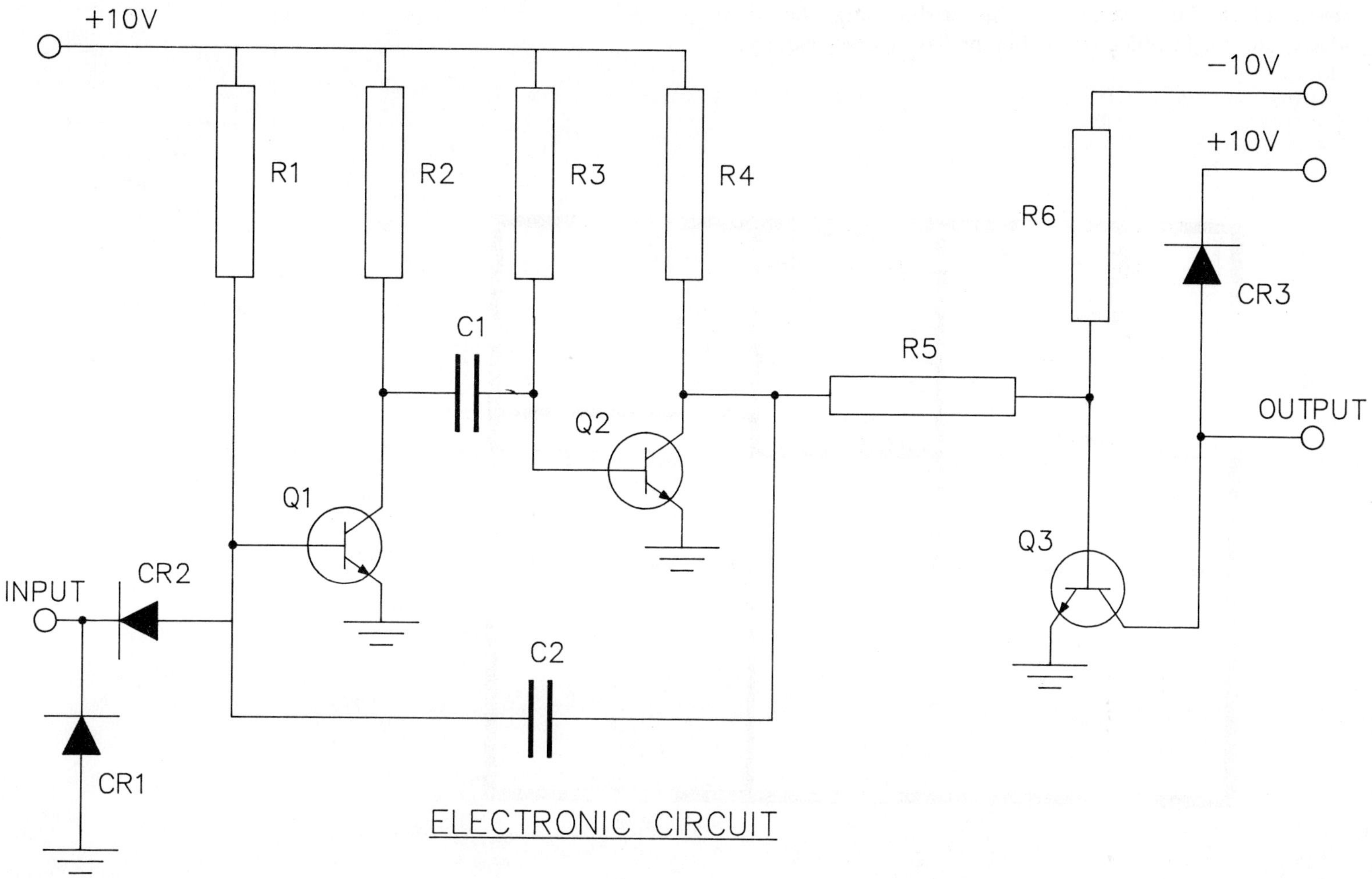

ELECTRONIC CIRCUIT

Tutorial 195

Tutorial 40. (1) Recall your drawing of the flat, i.e. **A:FLAT**. (2) Make some kitchen blocks of your choice (those shown are suggestions). (3) Design a kitchen layout. (4) Complete the design of the flat with more blocks for the lounge, bedroom, study, etc. (5) Produce two different flat layouts using your blocks.

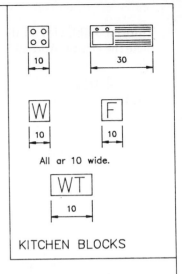

KITCHEN BLOCKS

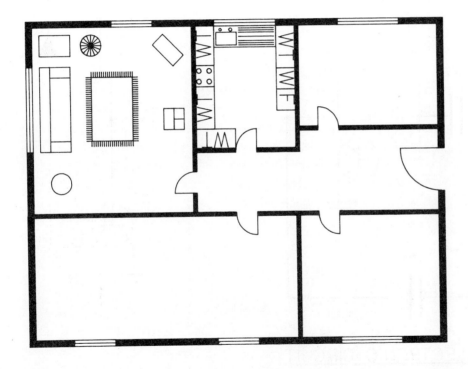

196 *Beginning AutoCAD*

Tutorial 41. (1) Draw the two views as shown. (2) Insert your **A:TITLE** block, in a suitable place. (3) Complete the title box.

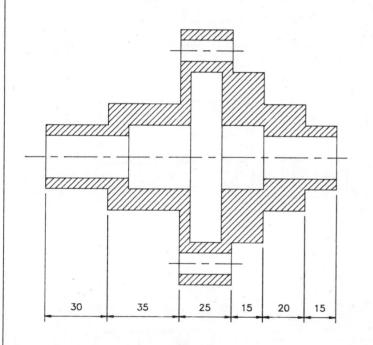
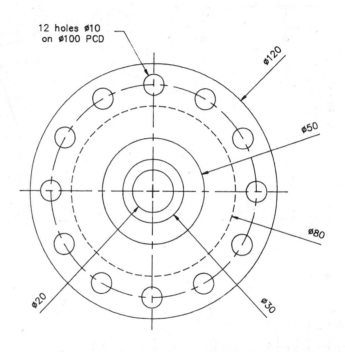

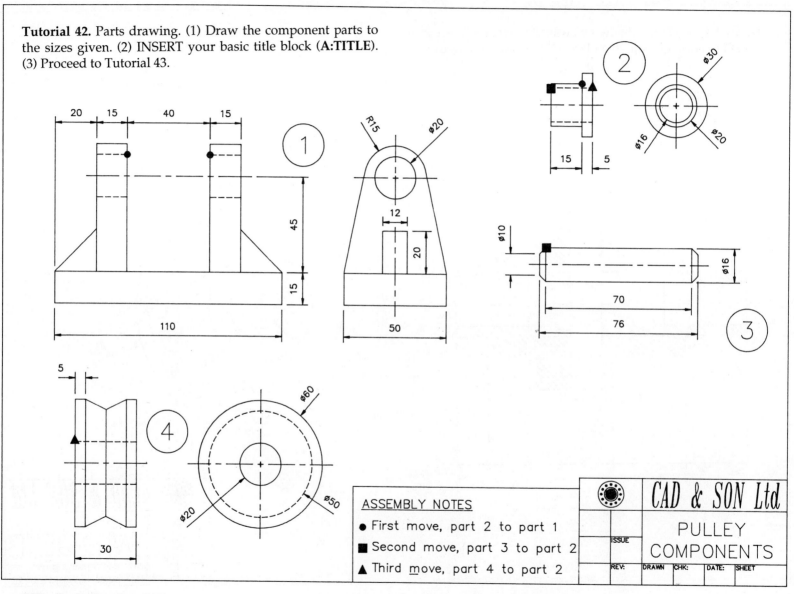

Tutorial 43. Assembly drawing. (1) Using the components from TUT 42 to produce the sectional assembly shown. (2) SCALE by 1.975:1. (3) Section using hatch patterns stated. (4) Insert the modified title box, i.e. **A:TITLEPL**. (5) Insert the parts list **A:PLIST**. (6) Add the attributes listed.

 ANSI31

 ANSI32

 ANSI33

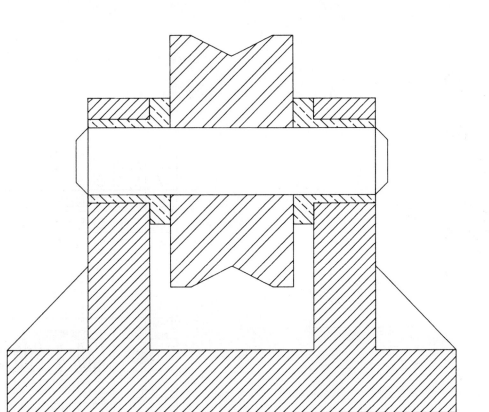

Tutorial 44. Detail drawing. (1) Draw the sectional assembly to your own sizes (the use of SNAP ON will greatly assist you). (2) Insert the modified title box (**A:TITLEPL**). (3) Insert the parts list (**A:PLIST**). (4) Add the attributes.

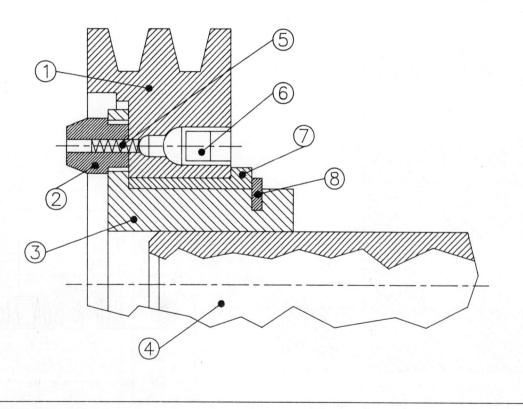

200   *Beginning AutoCAD*